THE WORD AS TRUTH

THE WORD AS TRUTH

A Critical Examination of the Christian
Doctrine of Revelation in the Writings of
Thomas Aquinas and Karl Barth

By
A. M. FAIRWEATHER

WIPF & STOCK · Eugene, Oregon

Wipf and Stock Publishers
199 W 8th Ave, Suite 3
Eugene, OR 97401

The Word As Truth
A Critical Examination of the Christian Doctrine of Revelation in the Writings of Thomas Aquinas and Karl Barth
By Fairweather, Alan
Copyright©1944 James Clarke & Co
ISBN 13: 978-1-60608-767-1
Publication date 5/26/2009
Previously published by Lutterworth Press, 1944

Copyright©Lutterworth Press1944
First English edition 1944 by Lutterworth Press
This edition published by arrangement with James Clarke & Co

CONTENTS

I. Introductory

(i) Until recently, Scripture has been accepted as a form of revelation. Karl Barth will not allow that revelation can assume such a form, on the ultimate ground that human nature is too corrupt to retain any divine gift. It follows that we cannot know the divine Will through scripture.

Revelation could not authenticate its source in God if originally given as propositions. It must originate as experience of God. So far, we agree with Dr. Temple's view but urge that truth which results from such experience is itself revelation, with its own redemptive value. The purpose of this essay is to argue that revelation retains its divinely given character and its capacity to direct the life of faith, despite its rationalization and transmission through human agencies, allowing revelation itself to explain how its human appropriation is possible.

(ii) Truth disclosed through revelation must be distinctive. The self-disclosure of God is not, however, peculiar to it. The theory of "preservation" may claim too much, yet God is significantly present throughout our environment. Creaturehood implies a permanent relation to God. Spiritual creaturehood implies a more significant relationship, divine influence being essential to the life of endeavour. The spiritual context of life can reveal itself. To deny this is a denial about God, not about man only. Hence natural theology is possible. What distinguishes revelation is the special self-disclosure of God, which realizes a new relationship of God to man and occurs because man's natural capacity to discern the already existing relationship proves insufficient for God's purpose.

(iii) God is not revealed as pure transcendence. Revelational knowledge of Him need not be specially deep or clear. The address of God is genuine, though its import be only partially understood. The certainty that it is God Who speaks is the only kind of clarity essential. By this certainty, revelation directly warrants the higher syntheses of thought (*e.g.* God is Love) as given, bidding us attempt them as best we can. In contrast, natural reason proceeds from less highly synthetic conceptions as given in experience to more highly synthetic conceptions as unverifiable conclusions. The difference is illustrated by the inevitably limited reach of W. R. Sorley's method of argument from "non-consequential" facts towards theistic conclusions. The movement of thought here depends upon the necessity of resolving the incongruity of the indifference of the causal order to the demands of conscience. But this necessity is ultimately dependent on the truth of the final syntheses towards which it appears to lead us, and can itself be maintained only as non-consequentially implied therein. By means of syntheses which are never final, revelation helps us to understand the divine-human relationship. Assent is to reality rather than to propositions. Paradox is a sign of the indispensability and value of the form of truth. (Note on Aquinas.)

II. Aquinas on the Origin of Revelation

(i) According to Aquinas, the function of revelation is to guide the thought of faith. Despite the suggestiveness of certain passages, he did not, however, believe that revelation originates in propositional form. His metaphysical system determines his view of how it can be given and received. There are two types of activity in an agent: one, "immanent"; the other, passing out to exterior things. God is revealed only by the latter, of which creation is the most important, producing "likenesses" to God in created things, by which He may be known. All human knowledge begins in sense, even of things that transcend sense. "Phantasms", received through sense and similar to material objects, are formed by the active intellect into "intelligible objects" connatural to our own level of being. These last are the true objects of thought, twice removed from the reality they represent. Aquinas recognizes that finally the mind refers directly to what it knows. But direct awareness is irreconcilable with his system, being seemingly impossible unless there is directness in the knowing process. With regard to the knowledge of God, the names we apply to Him may be applied analogously only, as indicating perfections which pertain to God in a more eminent way than is exemplified in the likenesses to Him from which they are derived. But it seems that concepts derived from sense cannot themselves supply this control over their application to God. Nor can they declare that God is a unity.

(ii) Aquinas conceives revelation as given through intermediaries, an "inner light" elevating the mind of man to perceive with certainty what is thereby revealed. Speech is not the bearer of revelation. The grace of speech is a gift to the prophet for commending his message to others. Though Aquinas at one point tentatively implies that apprehension of God may be direct, the ambiguous analogy of light does not succeed in reconciling this with the fundamentals of his system.

(iii) The knowledge of God thus explained has little beyond its own intrinsic value. Comprizing an authoritatively accepted assurance that certain propositions are true of God in a way we

CONTENTS

cannot comprehend, it lacks the moral dynamic which can only come from direct awareness of what we believe in. This limitation is inevitable so long as the hidden substance of God is taken to be the subject-matter of revelation. The doctrine of the Trinity is primarily an evangelical announcement of the way in which God has approached men, its significance as a doctrine of the divine essence being thence derivative.

III. GOD IN RELATION TO OURSELVES

(i) The Thomist system cannot take account of the direct personal approach of God, since it cannot allow a real meaning to "God in relation to creatures". Relations cannot pertain to God, either as substance or as accidents. But, for us, relations are not qualities of the subjects between which they hold. If God wills to relate Himself to creatures, such dependence of God on creatures as then obtains is not incompatible with His sovereignty, as can be explained by Aquinas' own distinction between asserting a proposition *in diviso* and asserting it *in composito*.

Aquinas considers the divine Love and Will as "immanent" activities only. The scriptures testify them as "outgoing" acts of God which achieve a permanent relationship between God and man. God-in-relation-to-ourselves would seem the only possible subject-matter of revelation. Though many questions are unanswerable, revelation realized as a divine-human relationship provides, by its own actuality, the possibility of its reception by man. The human reception of revelation is then the same event as its giving, viewed from the side of the recipient.

(ii) If revelation is thus achieved, two assertions impossible for Aquinas are justified. First, revelation affords immediate awareness of God. Unlike mediacy, immediacy of awareness cannot be demonstrated analytically, but proves itself by its occurrence. Certainty of it precedes the problem of how it is possible. It is more certain, if more inexplicable, in regard to persons than to things. The revealing acts of God are such as evoke responsive judgments of trust in which direct awareness of Personality is experimental and certain. Second, the names which revelation teaches us to apply to God may be applied directly, not analogously only. God is rightly described as the "Forgiver", etc., which He actually becomes in His acts towards men. We thus know God in the way He intends.

(iii) To a prophet or evangelist himself, the truth he leaves us would articulate and recall his own experience of God in act towards him. We must understand it similarly. "God is Love" must mean to us what it meant for St. John—the active divine

CONTENTS

Love manifest in Christ. We must also do justice to the process by which the truth reaches us. The written Word is God's address to ourselves through His original approach to others. The word as Truth is significant if it declares to us the conditions of our existence under God, and may thereby lead us to communion with Him. Barth's denials may be answered by defending the continuity of the process whereby revelation reaches us in the form of truth.

IV. THE BARTHIAN VIEW

(i) Barth insists that only the present event of God's speaking is revelation. The written Word is the witness that God speaks. Despite its inclusion in the threefold form of God's Word, it in no way expresses the content.

(ii) Some salutary warnings do not affect our view, which does not confine the aim of revelation to the giving of truth, and countenances neither atomism nor taking propositions *in vacuo*. We agree that the written Word must be understood in the spirit, but differ as to what this means. Barth holds that the written word is used instrumentally only, to bring us to revelation which it has no part in expressing. We maintain that it is used to bring revelation to us, defining what is spiritually received.

(iii) The several arguments by which Barth reaches his position are properly the divers expositions of an initial preview of discontinuity between God and man. They consequently appear to depend on falsely absolute alternatives between what is merely human and what is purely divine. The recurrent method of argument is to expose the former as incapable of bearing revelation, then to assert the latter as if the only alternative—intermediate views being ignored. This procedure is evident in F. W. Camfield's discussions on the "locale" of revelation and the "historic" Jesus. T. H. Green's principle that a higher agency transforms the significance of a lower, with which it combines, is outside the scope of Barthian thought. Hence the axiomatic certainty with which is assumed the negative principle that a worldly agency used by God cannot produce a result which remains attributable to God after His presence is withdrawn. This negative principle would justify all Barth's claims, but it is not self-evident.

(iv) We hold that the reactive contact of man with God issues in truth significantly attributable to God. Barth assumes that truth must be merely the product of our own "inner propensity". Since he does not examine the possibility of genuine reactive experience of God, he cannot justly estimate what may ensue from it. Though we cannot determine how far a human mind is conceptually operative in such experience, Barth's negations are unwarrantable.

(v) The anthropology which harmonizes with the principle of discontinuity is assumed along with it. In this connection, Barth misses the point of Gogarten's protests—which remain unanswered. Neither the status of man nor the nature of God's Word can be determined in abstraction from the actual speaking of God, which must be allowed to declare itself freely. We may accordingly call in question the presuppositions behind Barth's view—the presuppositions that sin has destroyed our capacity to hear God's Word and that revelation must be purely transcendent—before evincing the mediate character of God's actual speaking which we believe to justify our own. The mediate experience of God must be to some extent communicable.

V. THE PRESUPPOSITIONS

(i) According to Barth, the Fall affects both man and nature. Sin disqualifies us from understanding God's word, the true meaning of which is in any case destroyed by the forms of the corrupt natural cosmos within which we hear it. Unmediated contact with God in His absoluteness is thus necessary for revelation.

(ii) If the Imago were totally effaced, we could not recognize the fact. Barth places us betwixt impossibly narrow spiritual limits, as amenable to God's present act but not to His completed Act. Humanity is variable. We cannot put limits to divine grace. Sin prevents our knowing the divine essence and thereby determines the upper limit of the "locale" of revelation. But it cannot determine its lower limit. Grace reaches down to any depths it chooses. Sin need do no more than necessitate that God's Word be adapted in a form adequate for our condition. The divine indicative thus becomes an imperative. The problem set by sin is overcome by the unity of God with the worldly form of His Word. God's speaking is properly His, whatever its form. The moral knowledge of God, which Barth regards as valueless, is imperfect but nevertheless genuine and redemptive.

(iii) The sin of man provides an argument against, rather than for, Barth's second presupposition that revelation must be devoid of worldly form. Here, the question how real experience of the purely transcendent is possible presents an insuperable difficulty. Barth formerly sacrificed the reality of its human experience. His later compromise is unsatisfactory. In so far as Brunner tentatively allows that assent may be our own, he leaves assent on a different level from the experience of what it acknowledges.

F. W. Camfield's extreme position is inevitable, having recourse to a supra-rational consciousness, not ours but the mind of the Spirit. But the Spirit is generative of a consciousness which is our own, not constitutive of a consciousness other than our own. Regeneration implies continuity of the "new man" with the old.

(iv) The second presupposition renders an actively responsive fellowship with God impossible, whereas it is not precluded by the essential divine initiative. Barth's whole view supposes that God cannot speak to man without first negating the effects of sin, whereas the emphatic witness of both Testaments is that He addresses man in his sinful state. The worldly form of His Word is the only form then adequate to His purpose.

VI. THE MEDIACY OF OLD TESTAMENT REVELATION

(i) The experience of prophets permits of examination sufficient for our purpose. Theophanies may be classified according to the prominence of natural elements. Barth's distinction between an "upper" and an "under" in revelation is valid in a restricted sense only. Its elements are subordinate to a divine act as a whole, and a divine act to the attitude it expresses. But no further subordination is attested, the worldly form of revelation being unified with its content. Portent is sign merely, and represents the level to which Barth would reduce the worldly form of God's word. For this very reason, it is never the true worldly form. In Elijah's experience at Horeb the worldly form is properly the command of God, though the signs may be symbolic.

(ii) The point at issue in regard to revelation through history is whether historical events play any part in expressing a divine meaning. We hold they do so as involved in creating a divine-human relationship. The grounds for F. W. Camfield's contrary contention are insufficient, since God can make significant use of what is other than Himself. Events must be spiritually perceived. But their spiritual perception means the understanding of them in their full context, as acts of God; not the appreciation of a transcendence they have no part in expressing. The manner of the Spirit's inward working is not here relevant. The Old Testament provides overwhelming evidence that God's nature is understood through historical events and their circumstances. Though they could not explain the divine Will, concrete events may emphasize its inexorability, as is instanced in deutero-Isaiah and Jeremiah. The trust of the faithful is revelatory of God's way with men.

(iii) The condemnations of Amos illustrate how God is known as the abhorrer of particular human evil. His utterances are based on awareness of the moral continuum which embraces all humanity

CONTENTS

in a permanent relation to God, and upon which God's special Word builds a superstructure of grace.

(iv) At his call Isaiah is addressed in his normal state, his identity with his former self persisting while he hears the divine Word which is relevant for all and communicable to all. His natural faculties are not subdued in his experience of God, whose transcendence is manifest in recoil from worldly realities. Sin is not an obstacle to hearing the divine Word, but brings to light the full grace of redemptive communion.

(v) Jeremiah informs us of the ground of his right to speak for God. His naked humanity qualifies him to understand the mind of God as the enduring standard of right and wrong for all humanity. He is commissioned to deliver what he thus understands, as God's word. His own imperfect regeneration does not prevent him hearing God's Word, though it may interfere with the faithful discharge of his duty. Thus, in the Old Testament, the nature of God is declared through event, and in terms of human idea. It is a reasonable assumption that whatever limitations this mediacy imposes indicate the extent of the divine intention.

VII. How is Jesus Revelation?

(i) According to Barth, all revelation is identical with Jesus Christ. We may then ask "How is Jesus revelation?", in order to uphold at once the distinct contribution of the Old Testament and the revelatory character of the record of His life on earth. Barth's contention means that God's self-disclosure must invariably confront men with the precise fulness of grace manifest in Christ. "God's Word is God's Son." Though a unity is apparent in all redemptive acts of God, only Barth's view of sin precludes a progressive assimilation of progressively deeper revelation. Historically, if not logically, the Law is an actual pedagogue unto Christ. For Barth, only the transcendent aspect of Christ can be revelation. This robs the incarnation of its unique character and value. If its worldly aspect is not itself a significant determination of grace, the incarnation accomplishes nothing distinctively its own for the work of redemption.

(ii) Barth appeals to the Johannine writings for support of his view. But they neither affirm that God's Word is identical with God's Son nor confine revelation to the transcendent. In the Prologue, the precise identity Barth claims is precisely that which is lacking. St. John here proclaims the presence of God's creative Spirit with redemptive force in the Jesus who dwelt among men. The primary interest of the First Epistle is to declare, not the identity Barth requires, but the identity he denies—not that

God's Word is God's Son, but that the Jesus seen and heard of men is God's Son and Word. The aim of the Gospel is similar. It contains a series of signs which emphasize that the Christ after the flesh is the Son and Word of God. The signs are not external. Divine grace and truth directly confront us in the deeds which declare the Christ. The active manhood of Jesus defines the life of faith which God desires. Barth's absolute alternatives tend to confuse the issues.

(iii) St. Paul's teaching on spirituality is primarily practical, not a metaphysic of the Spirit's working. His love of the transcendent is natural to his temperament and understandable in view of his personal history. But no subordination of the worldly aspect of Jesus in revelation is implied by his insistence on the subjugation of the flesh and of worldly wisdom. Spirituality and unspirituality denote contrasting attitudes to the whole manifestation of Christ, not the appreciation of its contrasting aspects. The Christ after the flesh is revelation. The Spirit enables us to be persuaded of Him.

(iv) St. Paul's declaration in I Cor. xii. 3, shows that he discarded a view comparable with Barth's at his conversion.

The transfiguration is outside the general trend of revelation, which is manifest in and through the context of human need and endeavour.

VIII. THE IMPLICATIONS OF MEDIACY

(i) We agree that the Spirit is always a *dandum*, since it is God in act. Yet the issue remains as to how the unity of God with the written Word is possible. We differ from Barth in holding that no new outward act of God is necessary to this end. The Spirit must act inwardly, but the moral life is evidence that it always does so in some degree. Christian capacities are neither completely given nor completely withheld. St. Paul does not disown the capacity to preach God's word, but insists that this capacity is of God. St. John declares that the Word is extended through the fellowship of faith.

(ii) The evidence as to whether God's original approach can extend its influence through time is two-fold, respecting (a) how the Spirit works and (b) how God presents Himself outwardly. To some, the former may appear inconclusive. We have accordingly stressed the adaptation of the divine approach in forms appreciable by the human mind, which it allows to operate. God takes upon Himself the task of so presenting Himself that direct, though mediate, awareness of Him is possible to men despite their sin. It remains to determine what this means for the written Word.

CONTENTS

(iii) Since the divine approach achieves a divine-human relationship, the experience of which is expressible in words, the Written Word is properly a result of it. We must then show that this Word can convey the meaning which God intends and can be spiritually received as God's address. The truth handed down to us is instrumental as well as mediative. It causes the mind itself to act, while guiding its constructive thought. Because of our common humanity with the prophets, their testimony can guide our synthetic thought to appreciate the nature of their experiences. As creatures of God, we can appreciate in them their divine significance for ourselves.

(iv) The divine significance of the "demands" of God must be apparent if they are understood at all. Error in their reception by free minds is inevitable but not fatal. To guard against a fallacious "atomism", account must be taken of the historical context in which precepts emerge. Expressed for us in terms of human conduct, the Will of God is, so far, knowable. While Christ's example transcends our understanding, what God demands is the best we can do in response to it, and this is knowable. On a strict analysis, "I ought" implies "I can". We grow in grace through respecting character and conduct better than our own. Progress is helped, but not bounded, by the visible standards of a Christian community, which enables us to learn directly from Christ.

(v) Barth denies that the written Word can convey the "spirituality", "personal character" or "purposiveness" of God's speaking. He claims that only the present address of God can put us in touch with God as a Spiritual Person, since we cannot make contact with reality through idealistic thinking. Brunner similarly claims that idealist thought can do little more than set "data" in order; also that we cannot see through the events of history to the "purposive personality" behind them. We could not then meet with God through the record of His acts. The vital problem is not increased by the medium of words. Words are instrumental, and the limitation of their capacity to lead us to spiritual reality is properly the limitation pertaining to the human mind as such. Only in theory can data be isolated as barriers between us and the real. Reactive contact with the real is generative of them. Datum and physis are especially inseparable in regard to the historical, and biblical events are recorded because a purposive, divine Personality does show through them. The Spiritual God compels our acknowledgment in a two-fold way. He defies depersonalization as we contemplate His nature, while the Word is His present address to us now, even though it be the issue of an approach through the past. Processes of thought and concepts are the instruments of noetic contact with God, not substitutes for it.

The "personal character" and "purposiveness" of the Word are thus also safeguarded. The Word is intrinsically God's address, and could not otherwise be so much as a sign. Provided we adopt the fitting attitude of mind, mediative factors are irrelevant to its directness. Nor is its redemptive purpose obscured. To describe the Will of God as "general truth" is not to ignore its pointedness towards the individual but to recognize its universality.

(vi) The form of "truth" is essential for the adequate reception of God's Word as an address. We must articulate the divine nature, if only subconsciously. The universality of God cannot be adequately confessed save as a truth. Revelation appeals to the whole man. The need for an intellectual acknowledgment of God provides a distinct channel for grace. The Barthian insistence on God's direct presence and Aquinas' emphasis on the value of truth are supplementary.

IX. THE WILL OF GOD AND THE CHRISTIAN METAPHYSIC

(i) Recent circumstances have diverted attention from the formerly emphasized inward aspect of religion to questions about what God means for the world. In this latter regard, revelation discloses what ought to be the Christian metaphysic. As truth, the Word gives a knowledge of the conditions of our existence under God. As Will, it defines these conditions in terms of the conduct they demand.

(ii) According to Barth, divine immanence means no more than the possibility of the world becoming relevant to God's transcendent purpose, which alone matters and which we can serve only spasmodically when a special act of God gives the opportunity. According to Dr. Camfield, who discusses only the "limits" of immanence, with insufficient attention to its manner, the incarnation achieves no permanent relation between God and the world. The arguments supporting this point of view are answerable. God's free lordship is not jeopardized when He wills to bind the world to Himself. Nor must our relation to God be spasmodic, in any of its various aspects, merely because it is God Who achieves it. Fundamentally, Barth does less than justice to what revelation achieves. Providence means more than the possibility of our endeavours being relevant to its purpose. The Love of God in Christ began a new age. The forgiveness declared on the Cross is incomplete unless it reopens the opportunity to serve. Relevant service depends no longer on God's decision, but on ours. The Will of God, as known from Old Testament times, implies permanent and inexorable causal connections between obedience or disobedience to it and the furtherance or frustration of our good and the divine end. The attitude of Christ is evidence that our present world has intrinsic value in God's sight, though His supreme purpose lies beyond it. We serve His final purpose now if we attain a filial faith in furthering the well-being of the world we know, as included within the scope of Providence. The broad conceptions behind Barth's view are properly summaries of his verdict, not premises which might determine the limitations of practical religion. Only the Word of God can declare the possibilities which it opens to faith, thereby unifying the natural with the divine order.

(iii) The Christian revelation confronts us with our total spiritual environment, which calls for the endeavour of purposive goodwill perfected through communion with God. It teaches the attitude of Christ, the application of which to specific problems should become sufficiently apparent to purposeful inquiry. Though incompleteness and error are inevitable, providence implies that our endeavour is nevertheless significant. The enemy of progress is not uncertainty of God's Will but the deliberate violation of it.

(iv) Disillusion appears to be one cause of the preliminary despairing attitude common to Barth and Kierkegaard, whose theology is the reaction of an intense spiritual temperament to the impersonal religion of the rationalists. This reaction has less point where society is more placid and the Hegelian tradition lacking from our theological background. Barth's spiritual ancestry includes more than he claims. Manichæism foreshadowed the conception of a fallen nature and the consequent limitation of revelation to the transcendent. Luther is a forerunner in that he regarded human nature as too corrupt to co-operate with grace; Calvin, in so far as his view of sin excludes some from grace, necessitating a doctrine of arbitrary election; Jansen, in emphasizing the insufficiency of existing grace. The tendency to take dependence on God to mean that synergism is excluded in the reception of grace dates at least from St. Augustine. The teaching that self-despair must continue in the life lived under grace is especially Kierkegaard's. Barth could claim a closer affinity with John the Baptist than with either St. Paul or Jeremiah.

the interaction of the divinely illumined minds of men with divinely guided events of the "world-process"[1] We would agree further that the written Word, being conceptual, occupies an interim position.[2] It lies between the original experience of God which gave rise to it and our own appreciation of God which it may enable us to attain. But if it is allowed that human nature can receive and pass on anything of what it receives from God, it appears arbitrary to confine the term "revelation" to the actual intercourse of man with God, and to deny its application to the truth which is the outcome of this intercourse.[3]

If the word of truth is at once a gift of God and of practical significance in its conceptual form, it is surely justifiable to say that it is itself revelation, no less than the events which give rise to it. We cannot assume that it is not the divine intention to give us the Word as a divine gift significant in its own right. By its form of truth precisely it accomplishes a necessary redemptive work. Truth is one of the principles of integration by which personality is brought into harmony with the spiritual cosmos to which it belongs.[4] The Christian life, as an expression of this harmony, involves a maximum conviction of "what is", including a doctrine of man and the world along with its doctrine of God, and in its capacity of truth the Word gives us an understanding of the universe without which the practical life of faith could claim no rational basis.

The aim of this essay will be to show how the divine approach to men testified in the Old and New Testaments maintains its revelational character as a Word of God to us, despite its rationalization in the form of truth, and to urge that it is sufficient, by the claims which it lays upon us, to guide our endeavours now in channels relevant to God's purpose, despite the limitations imposed by the process of reaching us through the medium of human minds. In upholding these convictions we are at every turn dependent on the principle which Barth denies—the principle that men can appropriate divine grace by their works of faithful response to it. The nature of revelation itself must be the final grounds upon which we maintain that it remains with us in the form of truth, and revelation must be allowed to explain its own answer to the contention that the necessary human appropriation of grace is impossible.

2

Before proceeding to enquire how truth disclosed through relevation is possible, a discussion of its distinctive nature may

---

[1] Cf. *Nature, Man and God*, pp. 312 ff.
[2] *Op. cit.*, pp. 116–118.
[3] Cf. *op. cit.*, pp. 314, 350 ff.
[4] Cf. *op. cit.*, p. 237.

INTRODUCTORY: THE DISTINCTIVENESS OF REVELATION AS TRUTH

serve to indicate the view adopted on some recurrent controversial points. The truth made known by the revelationary process may be said to be concerned, broadly, with God and the continuum in which we stand related to Him. The natural reason may seek to discover this also, by submitting itself to reality as it meets us in normal human experience. We cannot say off-hand that knowledge of God through revelation is characterized by a divine act which makes it possible, and the discoveries of natural reason by the absence of any such act. It is only as the influence of the outgoing activity of God reaches us in some recognizable way that we can know Him at all.

The term "revelation" may be reserved to signify, as in its traditional usage, the special communication which issued in the written Word and is present in the Person of Christ; but if so it must be recognized that this need not be the only way in which God reveals Himself. The biblical witnesses themselves do not appear to deny that God can reveal Himself otherwise than in the ways they illustrate. We must not ignore the significance of utterances such as that of Jesus: "and no man knoweth who the Son is, but the Father; and who the Father is, but the Son, and he to whom the Son will reveal Him."[1] But the purpose of such a declaration is surely to point out the uniqueness of that knowledge of Father and Son together, and of the nature and identity of each in relation to the other, which corresponds to the uniqueness of Christ Himself, and which is only possible in and through spiritual communion with God through Christ as Son. The process whereby saving knowledge of God is given need not be commensurate with the process whereby all knowledge of Him is rendered possible. God may relate Himself otherwise to us.

May it not be that God has related Himself to us through the physical and spiritual cosmos, which is His own creation, in a continuously present relationship, and has done so in such a way that the natural reason can thereby know at least to a degree how it stands related to God, and therein something about God Himself? If this Self-relating of God to us is to afford a knowledge of God it must be charged with the power to reveal itself as what it is, namely, the self-relating to us of God and not of some other.

The theory of "preservation", maintaining that the permanent activity of God is required to sustain all creatures in being, would suffice for the permanence of the required relationship. But exception may be taken to this preservation on the ground that the act of creation is an act complete in itself once it is accomplished, and that there is no need for a continuous outgoing divine activity. Yet, even though we do not commit ourselves to believe in such a

[1] Matt. xi. 27.

statement concerning the activity of God, the permanent relationship may be maintained.

The initial act of God in creation must itself bring into being a relation of God to creatures which continues throughout the existence of creatures. Aquinas indeed denied this, naming it as one reason among others for holding the theory of preservation. "The impression made by an agent does not remain in the effect when the action of the agent ceases, unless that impression turns into and becomes part of the nature of the effect."[1] The necessary condition cannot be fulfilled when a superior genus acts on an inferior, nor therefore when God creates the creature. "What belongs to the superior genus in no way remains after the action is over."[2] But since we no longer think of creation as the bestowal on the creature of what belongs to the Creator, we may say that the impression made by God in creation does turn into and become "part of the nature of the effect". The act of creation cannot be without permanent effect. The created cannot cease to be created, and must continue in its creaturehood. If creaturehood signified only a quality of the created, in view of which we might contrast its internal character with some character of the divine, the creature could hardly provide the means of knowing God. But creaturehood would seem to signify, not the inner character of the creature in contrast to God, but the story of its creation. The term draws attention to the dependence in virtue of which the creature is and always shall be related to the God Who created it. If so, there is a permanent relation between God and all creatures.

When we turn to the spiritual world, the continuous sustaining activity of God may again be deemed superfluous. Even so, the initial act of creation must be of permanent influence on spiritual creatures no less than on others. We can no more escape from our creaturely nature than can inanimate things, and to be creaturely is to be related to the God Who made us. Yet the idea of preservation may be applied more acceptably in the spiritual than in the physical realm. The continuous outgoing act of God may be superfluous to our existence as creatures merely, but few theistic thinkers would deny that the continuous influence of God is essential to our life as spiritual creatures in the full sense of the word "spiritual". If the phrase "spiritual creatures" denoted only some character or characters obtaining purely within our created nature, which might be contrasted with the divine, this would afford no relation of God to us by which we could know Him, beyond that of the causality of creation. The category of causality, though enlightening in its own way, is so to a limited degree only.

---

[1] *Summa Contra Gentiles*, III, 65, 6.
[2] *The Word of God and the Word of Man*, p. 21.

INTRODUCTORY: THE DISTINCTIVENESS OF REVELATION AS TRUTH

But the phrase surely denotes more. The spiritual creature is what he is because he lives the moral and spiritual life of aspiration which is peculiar to his being as both creaturely and spiritual.[1] The good to which he aspires, which is ultimately God, is beyond him because he is creaturely. Yet he seeks it because he is spiritual; because there is in him a demand for an ultimate blessedness, containing within itself a promise of its fulfilment.

It has been abundantly argued that this seeking after God is only possible because of the initiative of God in calling man thus to aspire. Accepting this divine initiative as indispensable, we would note that it must mean a relating of Himself to us on the part of God, in a relation as continuous and abiding as is the life of human aspiration. Whatever be the complexities of this relationship, our creaturely spirituality requires the recognition of it. Man is the creation of a God Who continually calls forth towards fruition a capacity He has conferred. Man lives spiritually as he lives under the influence of this call.

If it be true, as St. Paul felt he could assume as a belief common to himself and the pagans of Athens, that in God we live, move, and have our being, then at every turn a relation of God to ourselves must be actually there. Further, since it is God who is thus related, the relation must be in some sense spiritual. In the words of Malebranche: "All the creatures, even the most material and, the most earthly, are in God as though in a quite spiritual manner."[2] And if this relation is abidingly there and is spiritual, it is only reasonable to suppose that it can reveal itself. God's relation to the world must be full of significance for the life that it sustains, and we cannot but suppose it to be His will that whosoever can at any time perceive it, through its significance becoming apparent, should do so.

Such a contention may be challenged, but only on the strength of denials which cannot, in the nature of the case, be finally substantiated. To deny that anything at all about God is discoverable from what man can perceive with his natural reason is not only a denial about man, but a denial about God. For it is to deny that God can leave any evidence of Himself in what He creates.

To deny that we can discover, from the moral and spiritual life of aspiration, anything concerning our destiny in God, may appear to be a denial only of the power of the human mind, but is also a denial about God. For if it does not deny that God's relation to us through the moral and spiritual continuum is a *real* relation of God to us, it at least denies the revelational quality of this abiding relation. We are not in a position to apply a general negative

---
[1] See A. E. Taylor, *Faith of a Moralist*, I, Ch. III.
[2] E.R.A. IX, 612, b.

either to the actuality or to the quality of any out-going activity of God. We can deny neither that He has permanently related Himself to creatures, nor that He has done so in a way that proclaims Himself, nor that He has created creatures who can perceive this permanent witness to Himself. Such a study as natural theology, which is entitled to take as the evidence on which it works the entire field of human experience, can claim, no less than the theology which takes its stand on revelation as traditionally understood, the guiding influence of the divine initiative on its thought.

Accordingly, revelation is not to be distinguished from the discoveries of natural reason by the presence of God's revealing relation to us, since this is always present. As the natural reason is met by the effects of the already accomplished relation of God to His world, this in itself is a contact of man with God indirectly, in which the mind is led to truth by God's influence. And since God's relation to the world is continuous with Himself, that contact may well occur with such clarity that it becomes a direct contact. And if there be this genuine meeting of man with God, the mind will then be led to truth not only by the impact of God's relation to the world, but by direct, personal contact with God. Such a contact will not be less than is meant by the personal address of God to man. It will be the present, particular speaking of God to this man here and now. It will also be as particular in its purpose as in its occurrence. The permanent relation of God cannot be intended to be directed to any particular person. But God's general purpose to speak in this way to such as may hear can only succeed, just as obviously, by giving enlightenment to a particular person. This general intent must thus become particularized as God's immediate purpose now towards him who has now found contact with Him. Such a contact, moreover, could proclaim itself as what it was, namely, the present speaking of God with revelational intent.

Thus, even without a *special* act of God, there may occur a *particular* speaking of God to man, with the purpose of giving enlightenment to him, revealing itself as God's act with this purpose. Such an event as this would seem to provide as direct a contact with God and as genuine a leading of the mind to truth by God's immediate presence as is possible. Need it be called less than revelation? We may say that a discovery of natural reason is then likewise revelation. There is then contact with God; God is immediately present to man's awareness; the immediacy of God's relation to man is the distinguishing feature of the process by which truth becomes known. It is at least a defensible contention that much of what is attested by the biblical witnesses as

INTRODUCTORY: THE DISTINCTIVENESS OF REVELATION AS TRUTH

revelation is intended by them to be understood thus, as the prophet's immediate and unmistakable meeting with God and His Will through the permanent relation of God to him in his normal environment, as a result of the use of his natural reason.

Compared with the special revelation attested in the Bible, the event above described lacks only the special act of God. In other respects the two are similar. Special revelation is attested as the coming forth of God in a *new* act, in which He speaks to a particular person or community at a particular time and place, always with the purpose of giving a particular enlightenment, and manifests that it is He who so speaks, thereby bringing into being a relation of Himself to man *which did not previously exist*. The very occurrence of special revealing acts of God must signify that, whatever be the revealing power inherent in the permanent relation of God to His creatures, it has in actual fact proved insufficient to secure such enlightenment as God requires, for His immediate or ulterior purpose. Only by the establishment of that relationship, progressively realized by the successive divine acts to which the Old and New Testaments bear witness, is the reality and significance of God sufficiently brought home to us. It is this self-relating of God to us which, beginning in the obscurity of past ages, realizes itself as a continuous development manifested in successive events on the historical plane, and culminates, though it does not cease, in the event of Christ's coming, which distinguishes the revelation of Christianity alike from other possible revelation and from the discovery of natural reason. It is this revelation with which we are concerned.

3

While God addresses us subjectively as Revealer, revelation always directs the mind to understand the nature of the God who speaks. Any fact about ourselves or our environment to which revelation draws attention must be a fact which counts in our relation to God. It must be significant in this way, if fit to be revealed by His special, purposive act. Whatever He chooses to reveal, therefore, God is at the same time revealing Himself. But God cannot reveal Himself by His pure presence. The human mind could not receive Him thus. Revelation cannot therefore direct our understanding to God Himself and quite alone. God manifests Himself only in and through what is not Himself, as God in continuity with some reality which we can perceive, and which is significant for our relation to Him. It is not then essential that the knowledge of God given through revelation should be deeper than that attainable by the natural reason. In neither case can God be seen purely and by Himself. In both cases He is understood as continuous with other realities of the continuum in which we live. A prophet may frequently speak in such a way that we must suppose him to have been given an acquaintance with God impossible to our normal state, but this is not invariably the case. Amos claims to have heard the special speaking of God with such certainty as entitles him to prefix his utterance with "Thus saith the Lord," even when its content concerns the simplest of human moral conduct and when the prophet himself gives us no apparent ground for supposing that he has been given to know God otherwise than as He who commands it.

Nor does it appear necessary that God's special speaking should be heard with a clarity[1] peculiar to itself. The perfectly clear reception of God's Word would mean that its entire import was clearly discerned, and it is difficult to maintain that it is so in any particular theophony. There are indeed commands attested as God's special word which seem incapable of being understood except with complete clarity, such as those dealing negatively with human conduct. "Thou shalt not kill" seems clear as to its meaning. But the command given to Gideon to smite the Midianites is the very reverse of this, and equally clear, while it is likewise attested as God's special word to Gideon. Nor can we altogether resolve the contradiction by remarking that the word to Gideon concerns only a single event in the process of history, while the former concerns a principle of perfected civilization, since the former is also a practical principle for the creation of such a civilization. If the two theophonies are to stand as revelation we can only conclude that God speaks in such a way that the import of His Word is perceivable in varying degrees, and that His special speaking, no less than the impact of His abiding relation to the world, is to be conceived as coming forth as a force compelling him who hears to perceive its meaning with the greatest degree of clarity which his human nature and circumstances allow.

Complete clarity of perception would mean the negation of all limitations of human nature and environment. If this occurred, it would render possible not only an exact understanding of the self-contained meaning both of God's Will for a particular situation and of His Will as manifested in the form of a principle, but also a clear perception of their import as God's Will. Real clarity would require this. To perceive clearly the Will of the speaking God in any manifestation would be to perceive that Will in itself, and to understand its single manifestation in relation to its entirety.

---

[1] As held by Brunner. See *The Philosophy of Religion*, p. 32.

INTRODUCTORY: THE DISTINCTIVENESS OF REVELATION AS TRUTH

So likewise with any particular manifestation of providence. Thorough clarity of perception would mean perception of providence itself, and of the single act in relation to the whole purpose of God become apparent. But the prophets and leaders of the Old Testament do not claim a clear understanding of God's ultimate purpose. Their trust resembles rather that of Abraham, who went out not knowing whither he went. What they were clear about was that God did have a purpose, and that certain events were determined for the sake of it by His providential acts. So neither does any prophet claim to have a final understanding of God's entire Will as it ultimately is. This would be possible only as included in the clear vision of God's purpose, since God's Will must be determined by His purpose, if not indeed in the last analysis identical with it.

Where the Will and Providence of God are not clearly known in themselves, the import of their particular manifestations as related to them cannot be clearly discernible either. And if clarity as to their import in this direction is not required for the attested reception of God's special speaking, why should absolute clarity as to the particular meaning which God offers to convey be essential? God's speaking will not cease to be itself if its meaning is discerned indistinctly rather than distinctly. If the prophet is brought nearer in any degree to understanding what God's revealing act has the power to convey, it will still be the work of this act of God that he perceives what he does, and what he does perceive must therefore stand as genuine revelation.

The test of revelation is surely not that the maximum light be received, but that something be received; not that everything be accomplished by God's act, but that something be so accomplished. And if the result of God's speaking is indeterminable in abstraction from the human nature and environment of the hearer, we cannot properly speak of exactness in discerning the import of God's Word, but only of thoroughness. So long as the mind is led by God's speaking, any articulation of its import will be in accordance with God's desire, and may in this sense be said to be exact or clear. At the same time it may be that no articulation is ever the most thorough possible, so that none can ever be said to be exactly as God desires it should be, nor, therefore, perfectly clear.

Thus the clarity essential to revelation does not pertain to its objective aspect—neither to the particular manifestations of God's Will or Providence as its immediate content, nor to God or His ultimate Will or purpose understood by means of them. In so far as divine realities are presented to us as objects of thought, their presentation must come under the limitations of human thought. In so far as the content of revelation is received as objective, it is rationalized; and the knowledge of divine things given in this way must therefore be, as rationalized objective knowledge, on a par with any knowledge of them, however gained. It need not therefore transcend the natural knowledge of God in any way in which rational thought is measurable, whether in point of depth, clarity, or any such measure. But special revelation is a disclosure in which God reveals Himself subjectively also, as Revealer, giving to the recipient the assurance that it is God Who speaks and none other. The clarity which is essential concerns rather this subjective aspect. The speaking of God with special intent belongs to no other event and characterizes no other truth than that which follows as the result of His personal address.

The clear conviction of the special speaking of God obviously makes a difference to our trust in the conceptions of things which it leads us to form for ourselves. We seek to understand the nature of the real by means of the combination and separation of ideas, and the propositional form of truth is significant in that it guides this double process of synthesis and analysis. It is the control and justification of syntheses which appears to be of special moment in revelation. The natural reason, following in the reverse order of being the relatedness of God to the world, must begin with such effects of God on the creaturely world as are immediately perceivable, and as may be met with in normal human experience. From these as given it reaches out beyond them to a contemplation of reality in a conception which is more highly synthesized than the data from which it starts. It may even begin with factual evidence which is not, on its own face value, apparently connected with the divine, seeking by interpretation to discover and define this connection in a highly synthetic conception of the whole. But wherever we place its starting point, natural reason must proceed, in its search after the divine truth of things, from the less highly to the more highly synthetic.

This not on the side of reality itself, but on the side of its own thought. God is a unity. His effects appear as a plurality. But God as an absolute unity is beyond the capacity of human thought to grasp, and from His effects we can seek to understand His unity only by synthesizing as far as we can the various lesser conceptions by means of which we articulate to ourselves the several ways in which His outgoing influence reaches us.

We may be given to meet with God in nature as Power. The enlightened natural reason may also, conceivably, be given to meet with God through the moral continuum as Love. But it is asking a great deal to suppose that natural reason meets experimentally with the unity of God as both the Power behind the universe and as Love. That the Power behind all being is Love is a truth which, if reached at all by natural reason, is reached by conception and not by perception. The natural reason depends for its warrant on what is given to experience, and advances by syntheses to a conception of total reality which is not warranted by an actual meeting with reality in the form represented by this conception. In revelation such a venture is excluded, for here it is not so much the elements of which the final conception is made up which are divinely warranted so much as the final conception itself. The elements of thought may be entirely our own. Indeed they must be so, initially, if it is to man as He finds him that God speaks, to whatever degree they may be transformed in the life of response, and hence one possibility of error in the hearing of God's Word. But the divine warrant is given to the synthetic use of them in the conception indicated by the propositional truth which records the giving of this warrant while it directs the syntheses of human thought—which assures us of God's speaking, the subjective content, while it leads the mind in the direction which God requires. "God is Love" is a synthesis which revelation commands us to attempt as we can.

Hence we may say that a real difference between truth disclosed through revelation and truth reached by natural reason, is to be found in the relation of the degree of syntheses in the conceptions which represent the given, to the degree of syntheses in the conceptions in which the mind finally rests and trusts. For natural reason the conceptions which represent the experimentally given are always less highly synthesized than those which represent the conclusions in which it rests concerning divine things. Revelation cannot leave the syntheses involved in the truth in which it bids us trust wider in reach than those which it presents and guarantees. If it did so, the construction of our conceptions would be our own no less than the material of which it is constructed, and there would be no leading of the mind to truth by God's Act. Here the syntheses of the world-view in which we believe are themselves the given. They may be either equal to, or narrower, but not wider than those justified by the original prophetic experience of the special speaking of God from which the truth is derived.

The significance of the propositional form of revelation in preserving for us the divine guidance of the synthetic activity of thought may be illustrated in contrast to the manner in which such a writer as W. R. Sorley feels bound to proceed when engaged in determining what may be said about the world in which we live without making use of special revelation. The form of the argument of "Moral Values and the Idea of God" is significant. Sorley feels entitled to take as given (as part of the material which we must take into account before we have the right to accept any philosophical theory as an adequate point of view for the interpretation of reality as a whole) two "non-consequential" facts.[1] One is the reality of the moral values as constituting a Moral Order, whose claim to objectivity is equal to that of the natural order. The other is "that the order of the world as a causal system displays such apparent indifference to the standard of good and evil."[2]

So far, we stand upon the witness of actual experience. But not so with regard to the reality of God, which must be reached as a "consequential" fact. This is accomplished by observing that the incongruity between the natural and the moral order cannot be allowed to stand as ultimate. We must attain a view of the universe as a whole which resolves the incongruity by explaining as reasonable the discrepancy presented to our experience, and the only way of doing so is to interpret the world as a purposive system; a fit medium not for the just rewarding of deeds but for the fashioning and training of moral beings, according to the Will of the Supreme Mind, or God, as the ground of all reality.[3]

The limitation of the argument is of course pointed out, and it would appear to be simply the limitation of the natural reason. The conclusion can be shown to be not inconsistent with the observable facts, but not to be positively demanded by them. But on what grounds have we the right to regard the apparent indifference of the natural order to the standards of good and evil as an incongruity which must be resolved? Why should this indifference be only apparent, rather than an ultimate fact of the universe; and whence comes the necessity of finding a point of view which explains it as reasonable? Not from the apparent opposition of the two non-consequential facts. That they appear irreconcilable means that there is as much experimental evidence on the one side as on the other as to the ultimate nature of the universe—that the facts of experience suggest to the intellect both that the power behind the created world is a unity with the God of Right and of Love, and that it is not so. Indeed the synthesis "God is Love", which expresses this unity, appears to reason a paradox as readily as it appears a truth. "That in spite of all the confusion and heartbreak and frustration of life, the sins, follies, accidents, disasters, diseases, so undiscriminating in their incidence, so ruthless in their working out, every individual may, if he will, not in imagination but in fact, rest upon a love which numbers the very hairs of his head—that is a conception before which the intellect sinks down in complete paralysis."[4]

[1] *Op. cit.*, pp. 501 ff.   [2] *Op. cit.*, p. 503.
[3] *Op. cit.*; cf. especially pp. 340–346.
[4] See H. H. Farmer, *The World and God*, p. 101.

INTRODUCTORY: THE DISTINCTIVENESS OF REVELATION AS TRUTH

There is nothing inconsistent in supposing that the natural order is in conflict with the moral. The principle of non-contradiction requires that our statement about reality be self-consistent, and in accordance with it we must remove oppositions which occur within our own thinking. But it does not require that we remove oppositions in the real. The indifference of the causal order is, indeed, a real one which the Christian Faith allows to stand as ultimate in so far as it arises from human sin as the ultimate, inexplicable source of opposition to God's Will.

The necessity of resolving the apparent incongruity, apart from the reality of sin, must be a non-consequential necessity. In the argument of natural reason, the incentive to venture upon a resolution comes from the one side of the opposition; from the demands of the moral conscience, not from the fact of the opposition itself. The demand that there be no ultimate tension between morality and the physical world is an inner demand of morality for its own sovereignty. While conscience includes this demand for the sovereignty of right, its validity could be completely demonstrated to natural reason only by actual experience of this sovereignty as an actuality. This would mean an actual meeting with God. To see how right is sovereign in spite of all appearances would be to experience the ultimate Power behind all being in its ethical working—to perceive God in His providence, and this would be to perceive all things together, the apparent facts, the activity of God who controls them, and God Himself in the one, undivided experience. Apart from the possibility of such a thoroughgoing insight into the nature of things, the maximum synthesis of the sovereignty of right must be a venture to natural reason. Revelation commands us to trust in the maximum synthesis "God is Love", which involves the sovereignty of right. And this divinely warranted synthesis, at one and the same time, invites us to recognize the indifference of the causal to the moral order as an incongruity, and provides us with the non-consequential necessity of seeking its resolution.

May not, then, the propositional form of the Word be allowed to stand as revelation? If it is through God's initial act that we are led by it in our constructive thinking about God and the world, it must be allowed so to stand, since what it accomplishes for us springs from God's act. To give us to comprehend how we stand in a permanent relation to God, already real previously to itself, would be a significant accomplishment of the Word. To give us to comprehend how we stand in this relationship now enriched by the Word itself would be more so. Revelation must certainly do more than provide us with truth. As the spiritual approach of God to the world it creates the enriched relationship the truth of which it presents to our minds. In respect of the purposive providential energy of God involved, this relationship must be real independently of our acquaintance with it; while in respect of its personal aspect it is realized only in and with our direct acquaintance. Our direct acquaintance with this enriched relationship may be the full intention of the Word. But if we can be led towards such acquaintance by being first given to understand its nature, the Word is then significant in its form as truth. To meet with it in this form is for many the first contact with God's self-manifestation to the world. Assent to its truth must then come from ourselves, for, as said by Aquinas, in the last resort our own reason must decide whether we accept even the truths of revelation as true. We speak disparagingly about mere assent to propositions. But do we mean mere assent, or assent to mere propositions? Mere assent is possible and ignoble. Assent to a mere proposition is a monstrosity which cannot occur. For if assent is real, the proposition has done its work, and it is the ontological reality itself, whose nature the proposition has described to us, that we acknowledge.

In the form of truth, revelation enables us to appreciate God by indicating how thought should proceed in contemplating His nature and His acts. We would not claim that the conceptions we attain by its help are final with regard to their syntheses, any more than with regard to the material of human thought which they order. On the one hand, the written Word represents revelation given initially to finite minds; and on the other hand we may not contend that what happens in our own minds, what we ourselves accomplish in response to its guidance, is an adequate expression of the Unity of God. We must acknowledge the limitations of human nature, whether it be the human nature originally addressed or our own. Any synthesis which the mind can entertain must fall short of finality, so long as human thought is prismatic. Therefore what God can give to our minds cannot be a final understanding of His own unity, but only a serviceable leading of our minds to understand Him by the essentially human way of never final syntheses.

Wherever the human mind fails to comprehend the unity of God by its own natural method of synthesis in such a way as to satisfy itself, paradox must appear. But such paradox is a sign, not of the falsity of the direction thus given to the mind, but of the limited power of human thought; and a sign, not of the futility of this method whereby God guides the intellect, but of its indispensability and value. It is a sign of its indispensability, because paradox would be of no moment if it marked a limit of thought which did not matter; whereas it is of significance because it marks a stopping place on a journey of thought which does matter. It is essential that we be led in the way of truth. And it is a sign of its value, because paradox marks a stopping place where the mind can find no rest; and because, when the coming of the Word brings us to paradox, divinely given truth has met us at the boundary of human understanding, drawing us to follow further in the paths of truth, though we be as yet neither able nor prepared to do so. By the very paradoxes and crises of thought which it forces upon us, the Word reveals itself as indispensable for our well being, not only as revelation, but as the Word of Truth precisely.

Such a view of what the Word of God accomplishes is at least in harmony with its function as understood by St. Thomas Aquinas, who is of traditional importance as an exponent of revelation in the form of truth. He held that the aim of revelation is to lead us to the closest acquaintance with God that is possible in this present life. Since the divine approach itself must obviously be considered in any attempt to determine the extent of what it can achieve for us, it will be relevant to take account of Aquinas' view of the origin of revelation.

NOTE.—St. Thomas Aquinas was born near Aquino in A.D. 1225 or 1227. He early showed signs of exceptional piety and joined the Dominican order in 1243. Somewhat slow in awakening, his massive intellect quickly developed to maturity and independence under the influence of Albertus Magnus. St. Thomas is important in the history of thought because he sought to reconcile the Christian Faith with the more recent thought of his age. Until his development of the thought of Albertus made itself felt, it was doubtful whether the Church could accommodate the scientific views of the time. Through Averroes, Aristotle had become better known to the Latin West, and this led to many unbalanced and extravagant speculations,; so much so that Aristotle was for a time proscribed. St. Thomas used Aristotle with discrimination and definite loyalty to the Christian revelation as he understood it, attempting to remove the sense of opposition between knowledge and faith, between reason and revelation, and to present a comprehensive world-view in the light of all the known facts of science and philosophy. He regarded the Greek and the Hebrew outlook on the world as complementary; the former representing what natural reason could attain to, the latter being the product of revelation. At the same time he replaced the Platonic tradition, with its tendency to blur the distinction between natural and revealed religion, by the Aristotelian, the schoolmen being quite willing to accept Aristotle as representing the final attainment of unaided human reason, his limitations serving to emphasize the need for revelation. Thus also the natural virtues of Aristotle were accepted as the foundation upon which the supernatural virtues of Faith, Hope, and Charity are superimposed. Aquinas held that the existence of God, His general providence, human freedom and responsibility, the natural virtues, and the immortality of the soul were discoverable by reason, but that truth peculiar to Christianity, such as the Holy Trinity and the Incarnation, could be attained only through revelation. Of the almost inevitable limitations of this greatest of mediæval thinkers to whom we owe so much, the following cannot but be apparent to those whom the reformation has influenced:(1) His uncritical view of the Scriptures; (2) His static view of tradition; (3) His "external" view of authority in matters of dogma, with its centre in an infallible church. A more closely knit synthesis of reason and revelation than that achieved by Aquinas becomes possible only when these views are transcended.

II

AQUINAS ON THE ORIGIN OF REVELATION

I

Whether or not we are disposed to admit that the propositional form of the Word is intended as revelation, it is certainly accepted as such by the plain man; and whether or not we are agreed that its work of directing the thought of faith is what it is divinely intended to do, it actually does this. As we receive the written Word now, the attention we give it results in the combination and separation of ideas along certain lines, whatever other results may ensue. It thus gives us truth, such as can be verified by experience in proportion as it deals with ourselves and what is near to us; and also such as transcends reason in proportion as it relates to God Himself, and cannot be verified by the unaided resources of reason.

Read in isolation, certain passages of Aquinas may seem to imply that revelation not only comes to us now as the guidance of synthetic thought, but was originally given as such. "Wholesome therefore is the arrangement of divine clemency, whereby things even that reason can investigate are commanded to be held in faith, so that all might easily be partakers of the knowledge of God, and that without doubt and error."[1] "Though human reason cannot fully grasp truths above reason, nevertheless it is much perfected by holding truths after some fashion at least by faith."[2] He speaks also of a "descent of divine truth by revelation to us; truth exceeding human understanding; truth accepted, not as demonstrated to sight, but as orally delivered for belief";[3] and of the knowledge of faith as "more like hearing than seeing".[4] And quoting Ps. 94: "The Lord knoweth the thoughts of man", he adds, "which certainly proceed by combination and separation of ideas."[5] To speak of truths as "commanded to be held in faith"; or of a "descent of divine truth"; or of those beyond our understanding as "orally delivered for belief" does suggest the original presentation of such truths in a ready-made propositional form.

But Aquinas did not believe in such an origin. In such passages he seems plainly enough to refer to divinely given truths as the outcome of a process, it being the purpose of God's original reveal-

---

[1] *Summa Contra Gentiles*, I, 4.   [2] *Op. cit.*, I, 5.
[3] *Op. cit.*, IV, 1.   [4] *Op. cit.*, III, 40.
[5] *Op. cit.*, I, 58.

ing acts that they should thus confront us. In the third book of the *Summa Contra Gentiles* we find a very different account of their original giving. Before examining it, we may first look briefly to his metaphysical system to see in what way it permits him to conceive of how God can act in revelation, on the one hand, and of how man can receive it, on the other.

According to the Thomist metaphysics, there are two kinds of activity in an agent: one immanent in the agent, and a perfection of his, such as feeling, understanding, and willing; the other, "passing out" to an exterior thing, and a perfection of the thing made and constituted thereby: as warming, cutting, building. Both these acts are proper to God: the first inasmuch as He understands, wills, rejoices, and loves; the second, inasmuch as He produces and brings things into being, conserves and governs them.[1]

We may note especially that the actions whereby God wills and loves are included in the first group, being "immanent" in the agent; not "passing out". Only production, conservation, and government are activities passing out to inferior things. In the end all God's acts are the same, being one with the unity of God Himself.[2] Yet the distinction is relevant. It is only through those acts of God which pass out to created things that the human mind can come to know God.

To us it may appear that the divine government is the most significant of these, since the order of things seems to speak of a providential government. But, for Aquinas, the knowledge of God attainable through the outgoing act of government seems to be of quite secondary importance. In so far as things are "good", they may on his view be said to reflect the providence of God, since their goodness consists in their subservience to the divine end. "But even though the very nature of things were known to us, still we should have but slight knowledge of their order, of their mutual relations, and direction by divine providence to their final end, since we cannot penetrate the plan of Providence."[3] It is creation, which continues as conservation, which is of importance. Aquinas conceives of all causality, including that of creation, as "static".[4] God's activity in creation is at one and the same time an activity of God and a perfection of the thing it creates and constitutes.[5] There is thus some kind of an identity of God with His creatures; an identity which is, however, only such as is indicated by the term "likeness". God acts to the producing of

---

[1] *Op. cit.*, II, 1. [2] *Op. cit.*, II, 10.
[3] *Op. cit.*, IV, 1.
[4] This explanatory term is used by J. Rickaby.
[5] *Summa Contra Gentiles*, II, 1.

His own likeness.[1] Hence we have the *"analogia entis"*, in virtue of which it is possible for us to acquire some knowledge of God. "The things of sense, from which human reason takes its beginning of knowledge, retain in themselves some trace of imitation of God, inasmuch as they *are* and are *good.*"[2] As manifold effects they reflect in their own diverse, inferior perfections the superior perfection of God Who is their cause.

Aquinas maintained that all our knowledge begins from sense, even of things that transcend sense.[3] The mind does seek to understand the substance or essence of things themselves, but "the mode of our knowledge of the substance must be the mode of knowledge of whatever we know about the substance."[4] It appears that, for Aquinas, the possibility of knowledge is ultimately to be explained by the "static causality" so fundamental to his thinking. It is to the degree in which outside things in affecting us through sense become in a manner identical with ourselves that they become known. How this happens is explained in Book II. Ch. 77. The intellectual soul remains open to receive definite impressions in the likeness of things that come within our observation. These likenesses do not come to us immediately as the objects of the intellect. They are received first as "phantasms", bearing a real likeness to things in their material state. Our active intellect then works upon the phantasms, turning them into objects of understanding. In doing so it raises the likeness which exists in the phantasm to a higher level, to a level con-natural with ourselves, so that we actually receive it as a secondary likeness, twice removed from the external object. The objects of understanding are therefore primarily created by ourselves in the very act of perception. They do not, as Plato maintained, exist by themselves.[5]

If the understanding is confined to the appreciation of "intelligible objects" which the "active intellect" abstracts from sense, it follows that all knowledge must be indirect, and never immediate. Yet Aquinas regarded the final reference of the mind to its object as direct. "Now the mind apprehends the thing, not only as it is in the mind, but also as it is in its own nature; for we not only know that the thing is understood by us, but also that the thing exists, or has existed, or is to exist in its own nature. Though then at the time the thing has no being other than in the mind, still the mind stands related to it, not as it is in the mind, but as it is in its own nature, which the mind apprehends."[6] Aquinas thus takes account of the directness with which we appreciate

[1] *Op. cit.*, I, 8; II, 11, 3.
[2] *Op. cit.*, I, 8.
[3] *Op. cit.*, I, 3, 12.
[4] *Op. cit.*, I, 3.
[5] *Op. cit.*, II, 77.
[6] *Op. cit.*, I, 79.

the reality of things outside us. But the direct awareness he allows seems to be confined to the result of the knowing process, and we may ask how it is possible for the mind to stand directly related to a thing as it is in its own nature, in the resultant knowing of it, unless it is also directly related to the thing itself as well as to its own concepts in the process of coming to know. If the understanding is so "tied to sense" that the abstraction from sense by the "active intellect" accounts for everything in the formation of the objects of thought, an initial direct awareness seems impossible. If, on the other hand, the understanding contributes something of its own in dealing with the "intelligible objects", in such a way as renders possible a final direct reference of the mind to the thing itself, it is not then true to say that knowledge begins in sense only. Direct awareness of things therefore, while recognized, seems irreconcilable with Aquinas' theory of knowledge.

The natural knowledge of God must, of course, likewise begin from sense. The mode of our knowledge of His substance must be the mode of knowledge of whatever we know about the substance, and of God we know only His effects.[1] We begin by apprehending indirectly, as likenesses already made to a level con-natural with ourselves by the operation of the "active intellect", the likenesses to Himself which God's creative and constitutive causality impresses upon sensible things. From these as intelligible objects the understanding "arrives by way of divers concepts to the knowledge of God",[2] by applying to Him the manifold concepts derived from sense. But in no way can the essence of a cause be known in its effects unless the effects be the adequate expression of the whole power of the cause.[3] What we experience, know, and apply in name to God are only likenesses so imperfect that they prove wholly insufficient to declare the substance of God Himself.[4] The names we apply are therefore to be predicated of God by analogy only.[5] We must have regard to the order of cause and effect. "In every name we utter, if we consider the mode of signification, there is found an imperfection which does not attach to God", the mode of signification being the mode of our knowledge.[6] Such names must therefore be denied of God on account of the mode of signification. But they may be affirmed of Him on account of what they are intended to signify, since this "may attach to God in some eminent way."[7] But, even in the analogous application permissible we indicate the nature of God only by negative differentiation from or comparison with other things. "But the mode of

---

[1] *Op. cit.*, I, 3.
[2] *Op. cit.*, I, 36.
[3] *Op. cit.*, III, 49.
[4] *Op. cit.*, I, 8.
[5] *Op. cit.*, I, 33.
[6] *Op. cit.*, I, 30.
[7] *Ibid.*

supereminence, whereby the said perfections are found in God, cannot be signified by the names imposed by us, except by negation, as when we call God 'eternal' or 'infinite', or by reference or comparison of Him to other things, as when He is called the 'First Cause' or the 'Sovereign Good'. For we cannot take in of God what He is, but only what He is not, and how things stand related to Him."[1] This application of names derived from "what God is not" to "God as He is in Himself" is significant, and not a mere "knowing of God what He is not"; since to indicate God's nature by negative differentiation from things is to indicate it positively. Thus the predicate "living" applied both to God and to creatures affirms at least that God is so far one with the living creatures we know as to agree with them in the negation of the inanimate.[2]

Thus, while the knowledge of the "what" of God's nature is indirectly acquired and inadequate, yet the mind, in applying its concepts analogously to God, understands directly something about God. Likewise also, "though our understanding arrives by way of divers concepts to the knowledge of God, still it understands the absolute oneness of the object answering to these concepts."[3] Some direct awareness of God appears to be necessary to explain the control which the mind must exercise over the application of its concepts: on account of the transcendent superiority of perfections found in God, on the one hand; and on account of the Unity of His being, on the other, as well as to explain the directness of the application itself.

Since Aquinas maintained that the reality of God as First Cause, and also His Unity, are demonstrable by reason, the natural reason being led to them by the apparent effects:[4] and since he denied that they are self-evident to us;[5] we must say, on his view, that the sense concepts from which we start themselves declare to us the necessity of controlling their application to God as described. It is difficult to see how they can do so. The identity which obtains after a fashion between God and the intelligible objects of sense may conceivably explain how the immediate awareness of these objects includes awareness of the necessity of distinguishing between the "mode of signification" with which they equip the mind and the "mode of super-eminence whereby the said perfections are found in God." Things could be thus explained if the "intelligible objects" could be said to declare not only themselves but their inferiority in comparison with God. But, if all this is included in their presentation, the mind stands initially related directly to God, and directly aware of Him, even

---

[1] *Op. cit.*, I, 30.
[2] *Op. cit.*, I, 33.
[3] *Op. cit.*, I, 36.
[4] *Op. cit.*, I, 3.
[5] *Op. cit.*, I, 11.

though it does so in and through the awareness of its own objects. So, likewise, it might be argued that this same identity gives to the manifold appearances the power to declare to us the necessity of understanding God as a Unity, despite their multiplicity. But here again the mind would be directly related to God Himself at the outset, even if in and through the appearances. And it would seem that this is only possible if in their multiplicity the appearances themselves actually express the absolute Unity of God. But it is expressly in this that, even on the view of Aquinas, they most obviously fail. They present us with diversity and not with unity.

The principles of the reality and unity of God as First Cause are probably most properly regarded as inherited axioms of the Thomist system, it being impossible to explain either them or the service they render to thought by a reference to the system itself.[1] They represent, not something that can be known of God by the manner of knowledge expounded, but the irreconcilable necessity of an immediate awareness of God on the incoming side of knowledge.

2

We may now turn to the account of the origin of revelation. Since revelation is given to man in his creaturely state, the question as to the manner of its origin is the question as to how it is possible for God to help man to understand His essence, considering his present state and circumstances. The account of it must therefore respect not only the metaphysical principle according to which God's self-revealing activity is conceived, but also the already determined nature of human knowledge. We find that, in the account given, the limitation of God's act to that of causality and the restriction of human knowledge to its beginning in sense are observed fundamentally with all seriousness; while direct awareness appears only as an element which cannot be entirely dispensed with. "Since the things done by God are done in order, a certain order had to be followed in the manifestation of the truths of faith."[2] "In his present state in which his understanding is tied to sense, the mind of man cannot possibly be elevated to any clear discernment of truths that surpass all proportions of sense."[3] The invisible good things, the vision of which makes the happiness of the blessed, and which are the objects of faith, "are therefore first revealed by God to the blessed angels by open

---

[1] See P. H. Wicksteed, *Reactions between Dogma and Philosophy*, p. 234.
[2] *Summa Contra Gentiles*, III, 155.
[3] *Op. cit.*, IV, 1.

vision: then by the ministry of angels they are manifested by God to certain men, not by open vision, but by a certitude arising from divine revelation. This revelation is made by an inner light of the mind, elevating the mind to see such things as the natural light of understanding cannot attain to. As the natural light of the understanding renders a man certain of what he observes by that light, so does this supernatural light convey certainty of the objects which it reveals."[1] Thus, Aquinas does not suppose that revelation is first given by the handing over of truths ready made. An utterance heard by the external senses or an inner locution is indeed said to be possible, but these are numbered among other possible but unnecessary "aids". "Without the inner light, these aids are insufficient for the knowledge of divine things, whereas the inner light is sufficient of itself without them."[2] The "grace of speech" is also communicated to the prophet, but this likewise stands outside the actual revelation, being given to confirm his announcements in the ears of others. The actual revelation is made by the inner light elevating the mind to perceive the objects of faith.

Aquinas strives at least to get as near to an actual vision of the realities in which faith believes as his metaphysics will allow. But we may ask how exactly we are intended to understand the operation of the inner light in giving the prophet certainty of these realities. In the above passage it is treated as one of the graces gratuitously received, given for the time being only. It is a special act of God which is causal in nature. It may be doubtful whether it is a new kind of causality or whether it is the causality by which God normally reveals Himself made more efficacious. Which it is depends on whether the elevation which occurs takes place as an event itself, leading to clearer perception, or whether the elevation is consequent on the gratuitous presentation of more perfect objects, or better likenesses of God, to the mind. But in either case the result is the same. The prophet is not brought to a direct awareness of the realities of faith, which is impossible, since not till he is delivered from the thraldom of sensible things can man be elevated to an "intuition" of revealed truth.[3] The elevation is only partial, and as long as knowledge is achieved through the sensible reception of God's causally transmitted likenesses, such elevation can never do more than give a direct awareness of better likenesses to Himself than we normally possess. So long as the operation of the inner light is conceived strictly in agreement with the principles already laid down, this is the only kind of "certainty" it can give.

[1] *Op. cit.*, III, 155.   [2] *Ibid.*
[3] *Summa Contra Gentiles*, IV, 1.

But in a preceding passage we find the analogy of light employed in a somewhat different fashion. In discussing how God can become known even to the elevated soul it is stated that, "if God's essence is to be seen, it must be seen in itself, so that the divine essence shall be at once the object which is seen and that whereby it is seen."[1] The principle of "static causality" can accomplish this in a measure, but not with sufficient thoroughness. On this principle, knowledge is explained as the "proper form" of the thing known becoming the form of the knower, and knowledge is possible only so far as this can really happen. The form of one thing can only become the form of another if that other comes to partake of some likeness to the former. It is then in proportion as our intellect, in partaking of some likeness to a thing, assumes its proper form, that we really know it. So with the knowledge of God. Some union of the intellect with Him is required. "If any created intellect begins anew to see the essence of God, the divine essence must be conjoined anew with that intellect by way of intelligible presentation."[2] Yet it can only be a union through partaking of likeness. "It is impossible for the very essence of God to become an intelligible form to any created intellect otherwise than by the said intellect coming to be partaker in some likeness to God."[3] The union can be effected by a change wrought either in God or in us. But God cannot change. The created intellect must therefore be given some new acquisition.

But how can this union be effected? As affected by the producing of a likeness to God in ourselves it is unsatisfactory, because of the obvious difference between a likeness and an identity. Aquinas then has recourse to the analogy of light. "That disposition therefore whereby a created intelligence is raised to the intellectual vision of the divine substance is called the 'light of glory'."[4] But its operation is scarcely consistent with his metaphysics. If the influx of divine light is to accomplish what is required in a manner strictly in agreement with its principles, it must bestow knowledge of God by creating an identity in point of being between God's very essence and the created intellect. But this, of course, is found to be untenable, and is expressly denied. By means of this light, the mind is declared to be conjoined with God, not in point of being, but only in point of understanding.[5] Thus, instead of overcoming the difficulty which arises from the difference between likeness and identity, and so preserving the tenability of the deposited theory of knowledge, the analogy of light really gives up

[1] *Op. cit.*, III, 51.
[2] *Op. cit.*, III, 53.
[3] *Ibid.*
[4] *Ibid.*
[5] *Summa Contra Gentiles*, III, 54. Reply to 2nd argument.

the principle of knowledge through the transmission of form. For if the mind is conjoined in point of understanding, but not in being, this is direct awareness of God in the acquisition of knowledge, the awareness itself being the new conjunction and acquisition.

Were we at liberty to understand the operation of the "inner light" in this way, it is evident that the original giving of revelation could lead to more serviceable results than Aquinas believes to ensue from it. For we should then be approaching a view of revelation as God's light shining, as it were, on the prophet, and so giving acquaintance with Himself. But we cannot interpret Aquinas thus. The intention clearly is that the light is not one which unites the prophet with God, but one shed upon improved likenesses to God's own Being. Revelation gives no actual meeting with God with Whom it is concerned.

3

We may then ask what service revelation given in this way can render us. Its function is to benefit us by giving certainty of the truths of faith. But it is obvious that we ourselves cannot receive the same kind of certainty as the prophet. Since we lack the elevation given to him, we cannot derive certainty of the realities in which faith trusts from these realities themselves, because our vision of these remains on the lower level con-natural with our normal selves. Consequently the revealed truths cannot declare to us their own authenticity as given by God.

In the end, our assent to their authority is won by miracle, the recorded conversion of mortal minds to assent to them being itself the miracle which best wins us.[1] But while we are won by miracle, it is the divine authority of the truths to which we assent that is the gift of revelation. It brings us to assent to its truths, which, while not contradicting reason, are beyond the capacity of reason to discover, and frequently to understand. But how much can yielding to this authority do for us? Its value is not intended by Aquinas to end with itself. In maintaining these truths after a fashion by faith we are given in this life as close an approximation to the final vision of God enjoyed by the blessed as our present condition will allow. But the value of this does not appear to lead to anything beyond its own actuality.

It is claimed that in assent to these truths the mental faculties are "evoked and led onward to something higher than our reason can attain at present, learning thereby to desire something and earnestly to tend to something that transcends the entire state of this present life; and such is the special function of the Christian

[1] *Op. cit.*, III, 155; f. I, 6.

Religion, which stands alone in its promise of spiritual and eternal goods."[1] In so far as the sheer appreciation of the reality of God in His own Being may bring with it a certain moral uplift, however inadequately His nature be conceived, we may agree with Aquinas that it is not entirely insignificant. But the rift between the direct reference of the mind to the objects of faith and the indirectness with which knowledge of them is attained here asserts itself as a rift between the spiritual goods promised and the assurance given as to their reality, and robs the direct reference of the mind to them of the moral dynamic this would otherwise afford. The assurance of them is given authoritatively, and the knowledge of them is nothing more than the formal assurance of their unknown, future possibility.

The Christian Religion does indeed promise spiritual goods unknown, but it also asserts continuity of our final inheritance with the earnest of it at present given to faith. Faith is already a communion with God, the final state of grace being this same communion perfected. A moral dynamic arises from the partial realization of the inheritance itself, the presence of God to us now inspiring us to strive for a closer acquaintance with Him. But with Aquinas the moral dynamic does not come from this communion itself. Rather must we say that the partial realization of blessedness remains an effect only. At least, in so far as it becomes causal it has left the presence of God behind. The sole presence of God to us is that which comes as the authority to which we assent in accepting truths. The achievement of revelation ends with the intrinsic value of the perfection attained in accepting them.

And when we assent to these truths what exactly do we do? We form for ourselves, by our own feeble syntheses, a proposition: and admit, on the one hand, that this is somehow true of God in a way we cannot understand; and, on the other, that nevertheless it is God's Will that we should think about Him thus. This substitution of authority for logical certainty cannot do more for us than could logical certainty itself. Certainty of truth cannot do more than bring us to acquaintance with the reality with which truth is concerned, and it can do this only if such acquaintance is itself possible.

From the start, the truths of revelation as set forth by Aquinas are separated from their subject-matter; and therein lies the fundamental limitation to their usefulness. Their subject-matter is the substance of God, of which we can have no direct knowledge in our present life. Revelation is not here concerned with itself, the approach of God to the world, and consequently cannot lead us to this approach. On the contrary, its truths appear as purely

[1] *Op. cit.*, I, 5.

"horizontal" propositions (as contrasted with the Barthian "perpendicular"), propositions about God in His own Being, about God in His hiddenness; not about God as He touches us, but about His substance as this does not affect us.

Even the doctrine of the Trinity becomes a doctrine about God in His own nature; so that the revelation of God as Father, Son, and Holy Spirit would be the better received could we better understand how the three Persons are related within the Godhead. Wherefore this doctrine remains altogether beyond human understanding, with insuperable difficulties in giving consistent expression to its meaning.[1] The doctrine of the Trinity may be by now a doctrine of God's essence, but there is no evidence that it began as such, and on the authority of the scriptural records we must acknowledge that the evangelists who gave us the doctrine did not so receive it. Its form as a doctrine of this kind is a subsequent articulation of what the evangelists found themselves compelled to say about God as the result of His actual approach as Son and as Spirit. Since the doctrine issues from the experience of the Personal approach wherein it is Himself, as thus communing with man, that God is concerned to reveal, it must be this approach that the doctrine properly affirms. Consequently, we are going beyond the intention of revelation, and also reversing the order of things, when we seek to understand or define the relations between Father, Son, and Spirit from within the doctrine of the Trinity. Rather is the doctrine itself to be defined by the events of the Son and Spirit.

Without the approach of God as their basis, propositions concerning God's nature cannot have a revelational value. Preceded by such an approach and asserted on the strength of it they may be significant enough. That Aquinas could not make room for such an approach must be attributed to the circumstance that he seeks to determine how God meets with man according to the possibilities allowed by his metaphysics, not from the witness of those to whom such a meeting was given. How their witness entitles us to regard the giving of Revelation, and how in consequence we must understand the status and significance of its truths, will be our next enquiry.

[1] See *Reactions between Dogma and Philosophy*, I, p. 273 ff.

III

GOD IN RELATION TO OURSELVES

I

The prophets certainly do seem to bear witness to such an approach of God to themselves as affords immediate awareness of Him. As we have seen, Aquinas cannot take account of such revelation because his theory of human knowledge, which rules out any immediate experience of God, means that a direct personal approach could not be received. But, for Aquinas, it is also impossible on God's side that revelation should be given in this way. For if God presents Himself to man through a personal approach, this means that He brings Himself into a real relationship with man, making Himself known through this self-relation; and Aquinas finds he is bound to deny that "God in relation to creatures" means anything real at all. The self-revelation of God through His immediate presence to us being thus doubly impossible for Aquinas, since it can neither be given nor received, we must now argue that it is at least not impossible, by showing that "God in relation to creatures" has a real meaning. We will then be free to accept the prophets' witness to the actuality of the divine self-relation, which in the end must explain its own possibility.

We may first observe how Aquinas comes to deny that "God in relation to creatures" means anything real. The question of how relations pertain to God follows from the discussion of the nature of God's activity, particularly with regard to the divine power. It is found that something must be predicated of God in regard to the effects which He produces. It is thus that we predicate "power" of Him. We do so as if power were a separate quality in God which enables Him to act. But it is not really a separate quality. There is in God only the action by which He produces, and His power is properly identical with His action.[1] We, because of our way of viewing things, view God's action under two aspects: calling it power as well as action.[2] When we view God's action as power, we predicate something of God in relation to other things. But we call His action "power" only because it appears to us to be this when we view Him and His effects together, holding them in relation to each other in our own minds. The predication of such relations arises only from a necessity of thought, and relations so

---
[1] *Summa Contra Gentiles*, II, 9.
[2] *Op. cit.*, II, 10.

predicated do not really pertain to God at all.[1] Aquinas evidently regarded all relations predicated of God in regard to creatures as attributed to Him in this way. We seem to be predicating relations themselves of God, when the relations we name properly represent only the movement of our minds as they contemplate two things at once. Likeness, knowledge in God, and what is especially relevant, God's firstness and sovereignty, are regarded in this way. "Whatever is first and sovereign is so in relation to others. But God is the first being and the sovereign good",[2]—wherefore God's sovereignty is nothing real about Himself.

Aquinas then proceeds by further argument which illustrates how the relations of God to creatures can never be conceived as real so long as thought is dominated by the conceptions of substance and accident as if these categories were exhaustive. "Relations cannot be in God as accidents in a substance, seeing that in God there is no accident. Nor again can they be the very substance of God. For then the substance of God in His very essence would be referred to another; but what is referred to another for its very essence in a manner depends on that other, as it can neither be nor be understood without it. But this would make the substance of God dependent on another being, foreign to itself."[3] Being possible neither as substance nor as accident, relations cannot be in God. But it is also impossible for the relations, whereby God has relation to the creatures, to be anything outside God.[4]

It is argued that while we may denominate a thing from something outside itself, in the case of relations we do not do so. Relations denominate a thing only as from something within itself. Thus, a man is not called "father" except from the paternity that is in him. Hence, since the relations of God to creatures cannot be outside Him and are not really in Him, and yet are predicated of Him, the only possible conclusion is that they are attributed to Him merely by our mode of thought. It is true that other beings are related to God. But it is not true that He is related to them. Thus relations are not to be predicated of God in the same way as other things. Other things, such as wisdom and will, are predicated of God's essence. But relations are only conceptual, according to our mode of thought. Aquinas adds, rather surprisingly, that our thought is nevertheless not at fault, for, by the very fact of our mind knowing that the relations of effects of divine power have God Himself for their term, it predicates some things of God relatively.

It is evident that, from first to last, Aquinas is not dealing with a "relation" as we would understand it. By a relation we would

[1] *Op. cit.*, II, 10.
[2] *Op. cit.*, II, 11, 3-5.
[3] *Op. cit.*, II, 12, 1.
[4] *Op. cit.*, II, 13.

understand something which obtains objectively between two realities as its terms, and if we do predicate a relation of one reality only we are really affirming that it holds between two; the relation being unaffected by our electing to define it from one of its terms, as the focus of our present interest, in preference to the other. But, for Aquinas, a relation is something within one reality. This is made plain when it is said that a man is called "father" only from the paternity that is in him; the term "father" indicating some inner quality of a man's being, not something he is made to be by the context of his environment.

In predicating relations of God we ought, therefore, on Aquinas' view, to be affirming something about God, as He is purely within Himself, which of course we can only do by "analogous" predication. So long as it is held that all affirmations about God are concerned with His substance, or with God as He is in Himself, relations cannot be properly predicated of Him. To be real, they would have to be identical with the divine substance, a *"res"* within the Godhead.[1] And, if the relations of God to creatures were real, their reality would at once render God's substance dependent on creatures for its very being, thus destroying the independent self-identity of God. But the relations of God to creatures as we would understand them, as obtaining objectively between God and creatures, and arising out of God's own free and active self-relation to them, do not destroy the divine independence. To use the distinction elsewhere used by Aquinas himself, the statement that "God is dependent on creatures" need be asserted *"in composito"* only; not *"in diviso"*.[2] If we had to make this statement *"in diviso"*; that is, absolutely, considering only one element in the proposition, namely "God", the divine independence would be lost. Relations could not then be real, since in His initial being God cannot be dependent on creatures. But we need say that God is dependent on creatures *"in composito"* only. That is, taking all elements in the situation into account, we must say that by His own will God has brought Himself into relation with creatures, and without this would not be what He now is, wherefore He has made Himself dependent on creatures in the manner which this implies, which destroys neither His self-identity nor freedom, since it is only the consequence of His own will and act.

For Aquinas, to assert the dependence of God on creatures *"in composito"* is nothing different from asserting it *"in diviso"*, because there is nothing further to take account of besides God in His own substance. He does not take account of the approach by which God relates Himself to man. We ought not to say that the

---

[1] Cf. *Reactions between Dogma and Philosophy*, p. 274.
[2] See *Summa Contra Gentiles*, I, 67, 8; and II, 25.

idea of such an approach of God is outside Aquinas' interest, but rather that since his interest in the *Contra Gentiles* is directed towards unbelievers he confines himself to the ground common to himself and to them, which is the philosophical ground. The approach of God must be unpredictable to any philosophical system, since it is God's special act, and the sole ground of its own possibility.

Following his metaphysics only, and not the biblical witness, Aquinas considers the Love and Will of God solely as "activities immanent in the agent." He cannot take account of them as the attested outgoing acts by which God reveals Himself, and consequently does not consider the possibility of a direct knowledge of God given through them. But the active approach by which God relates Himself to man is the very thing of which we must take account in dealing with the special revelation with which we are concerned. The whole story of revelation, the import of the history of Israel, the burden of the prophets, and the significance of the Person and teaching of Christ, is that God's Love and Will are outgoing acts of God towards us. It is expressly in them that God's self-giving is achieved, and through them that His nature is learned. To the Hebrew and the Christian believer alike, God's Love is not primarily something about God in His own essence, but is His Love toward mankind. In the Old Testament it appears as the divine guardianship over His chosen nation throughout their history for the sake of His own purpose. When the people are recalled by a prophet from recurrent disloyalty, it is in the God Who has actually and actively cared for them, named repeatedly as He who led them out of the land of Egypt, that they are called once more to place their trust. The Love of God, conceived in varying degrees of dignity and naïvety, and with many variations between complete universality towards the whole race of man and complete specialization towards themselves, is indeed a major distinguishing feature of the Hebrew religion. And when we turn to the Incarnation, we cannot say less than that Jesus Christ, in His Person and His works, is the advent of the divine good-will to men. Similarly with regard to the Will of God. The divine act by which God wills must be real in itself, but it is not a matter of revelation. The Will which is revealed is not an act which finds its term within God's being, but is His Will toward man, finding its term in man. It comes not as a fact about God's essence, but as a command which reaches those addressed as an event. It is revealed as a divine "thou shalt", or "thou shalt not"; as a personal approach of God as absolute demand[1] if it is anything at all.

[1] See H. H. Farmer, *The World and God.*

THE WORD AS TRUTH

The Love and Will of God, manifested in actual events of divine preservation, commandment, judgment, forgiveness and reconciliation, are undoubtedly understood as creating and constituting a permanent relation of God to his creatures. It is repeatedly the burden of a prophet to point out that, whether it be respected or disregarded, the relationship of God to His chosen nation is a fundamental and for ever inescapable fact about their existence. Christ's labour as Prophet is likewise to proclaim the Love of God perfected in Himself as the fundamental fact about all human existence; and to bring men to realize how they actually do stand toward God, because God, now in perpetuity and irrevocably, stands as He does toward them. We may then say that, while no revelation occurs without an actual visitation of God-in-act, the diverse acts of outgoing Love and Will by which God reveals Himself progressively realize and enrich a relationship or spiritual continuum in which God and man stand united to each other. The real subject-matter of revelation would thus seem to be the very thing which Aquinas could not admit to be real in itself, namely God in relation to ourselves, His permanent relationship being at once realized and revealed by the divine activity of which Thomist metaphysic does not take account, namely, by the particular expressions of God's outgoing Love and Will. The subject-matter may be said to include both the divine acts themselves and also whatsoever of the nature of God is understandable by means of them.

This indeed would seem to be the only subject-matter which can possibly be revealed. On the one hand, we could not receive a revelation of God in His own essence. On the other hand, the revelation of God must be a divine reality, since otherwise it would not be God that is revealed. Only God can reveal God; wherefore it must be God Himself Who meets us in revelation. The only way in which the achievement of this contact seems possible is through divine acts, which at once reach us by issuing in events in our own worldly environment and at the same time reveal themselves for what they are, as God's acts precisely. How exactly these acts of God are made known for what they fully are, whether it be that the outward events are directed with special force to the prophet's mind so that their origin in God becomes apparent to him, or whether he is stirred by some additional divine energy to perceive their full significance, must be to some extent an unanswerable question.

The inward energy of the revealing acts of God must ultimately be unanalysable. We shall have occasion later to examine this, so far as the nature of the case allows, but here we need only suppose that by God's act the prophet is taken into a spiritual communion with God in which he is given to see the outward events as God's acts, and in which the spiritual continuum between God and man which they realize and express is forced directly upon his awareness. Conceived as occurring thus, revelation provides, by its own actuality, and by this alone, the possibility of its own reception by man. The whole revealing act of God is the address of what God does and of what He thereby is, to the person to whom He speaks, and the awareness of this approach is itself part of the relationship realized between God and man. The human understanding of God's revealing act for what it fully is, is itself the very thing in which that revealing act terminates. When God reveals Himself through preserving and sustaining a prophet's courage and faith through times of affliction, as He is frequently declared to do, the prophet actually is sustained by God as Preserver of his faith. When God forgives and reconciles any person to Himself, such a one actually is forgiven by and reconciled to God. The human reception of revelation is the same thing as its giving. Whether we speak of the giving or of the receiving of revelation, we speak of one and the same relationship which God has somehow made real, defining this in two different ways, from God or from man as from one or other of its terms.

2

If revelation is achieved through the approach of God in His acts, two assertions may be made which were impossible for Aquinas.

First, that revelation affords immediate awareness of God; and second, that it gives real knowledge of God, Who is truly described by the names which it teaches us to apply to Him. If we consider the providential acts of God in history, others besides the prophet may stand directly related, in point of understanding, to the outward effects of God's act which belong to the historical plane. But when these effects are manifest to the prophet for what they fully are, he meets not only directly with the effects but with the divine act as such, and with God Himself as thus active. Nothing less than the immediate awareness of God, His act, and the outward worldly event as one undivided whole, would suffice to manifest any worldly event as unmistakably the work of God.

This direct awareness of God may be difficult to defend and to explain, but it is not for this reason impossible. While we can demonstrate mediacy by pointing to definite factors which seem to interpose between our minds and the things we know, immediacy is the absence of any obstruction to direct awareness, and cannot therefore be demonstrated in this way. It can only prove itself by its occurrence. But this it does, and in any analysis of knowledge it has a right to be considered as a basal fact equally with the other factors in the knowing process which may seem to preclude it. In the knowledge of a material object our *sensa* obviously form an intervening element, but at the same time we know not our *sensa* but the object itself, and we are aware that it is the object that we know. How we do this may be a problem we cannot solve. But we do not deny the fact on that account.

With regard to our knowledge of persons, immediate awareness of them is still more undeniable, if still more of a problem. The mediating factor of sense is quite incapable of explaining our awareness of them. And while it is undoubtedly because we are living persons ourselves that we are able to conceive what another personality must be like, yet our knowledge of our own nature is not the mediating factor which brings to us the awareness of another personality. Another person must be there before we apply concepts drawn from our self-knowledge in appreciating the personality which confronts us. The mediation which counts would seem to be that of the person's actions towards us, together with our response to them which they awaken; and these factors, though mediative, do not obstruct direct awareness, but rather the reverse. As said by Prof. Karl Heim and quoted by L. W. Grensted: the only judgment which has complete and irrefutable certainty is the judgment of trust.[1] We know a friend most thoroughly when we discover him to be trustworthy, and through our trusting him.

Why should it not be likewise between God and His prophet? God's acts as Guide, Preserver, Forgiver and Reconciler are of the very kind by which personality directly declares itself, and evoke as the fitting response to them that trust through which direct awareness is achieved with the greatest certainty.[2] The prophet's experience of being guided, sustained, or forgiven by God are not awareness of something other than God by means of which he knows God indirectly, but the manner of his direct acquaintance with God. His awareness of God is thus immediate while it is mediate, and mediate while it is immediate. It is only because it is immediate that it is real acquaintance; and it is only because it is mediate in the way in which it is so that its immediacy is possible. It is because his experience is his own, and because God's forgiving him is identical with his being forgiven by God, that he knows the forgiving God experimentally. When we speak of the knowledge involved in the reception of revelation, we are, of course, making an abstraction from what is a living contact. In the actual

[1] *The Person of Christ*, pp. 17 ff.; cf. *The World and God*, p. 19.
[2] Cf. H. R. Mackintosh, *The Christian Apprehension of God*, pp. 51 ff.

experience of which it is an abstraction, awareness is a practical and spiritual certainty, not a logical certainty.[1] It may be neither complete nor yet perfect, so far as it goes, but it is nevertheless immediate, because experimental. Imperfect awareness is quite compatible with immediate awareness.

Second, Aquinas asserts that names applied to God in His own essence can be applied analogously only.[2] They can never represent more than an inadequate comparison, or even contrast, between the creaturely and the incomprehensible divine nature. But if the subject-matter of revelation is not God, but God-in-relation-to-ourselves, the names which revelation teaches us to apply to God may truly describe Him. When we apply names to God in consequence of His self-relation to us, then just as the term "creaturehood" applied to ourselves indicates not some quality in us in contrast to the divine, but our creation by the divine together with what this entails, so the names applied to God describe not His essence in contrast to the creaturely but what He has actually done, and what He has thereby made Himself to be towards us. They describe the revelation which teaches us to use them. God is Preserver, Commander, and Judge because He preserves, commands, and judges; Forgiver, Reconciler, and Redeemer, because He forgives, reconciles, and redeems. Such names are therefore correctly predicated of God. It is true of God that He is all that they imply because He actually does all that they signify. We do not know the transcendent essence of God, but precisely in so far as this observation is true it is of no moment, since God's unrevealed essence is precisely what He is not concerned to reveal to us. But we do know God in relation to ourselves. This is His revealed nature, what He makes Himself to be by His purposive self-revelation, and what He is concerned that we should know about Him. We may note, finally, that, when we speak of God as first and sovereign in the manner in which revelation demands that we should, we are to a large extent simply repeating the assertion of God's approach to us as final demand. God is sovereign not in Himself for His own sake, but towards us for the sake of His purpose.[3]

3

We may now consider how such an origin affects the significance of revelation in the form of truth, which is the form in which it

---

[1] *Op. cit.*, p. 45.
[2] Cf. *Summa Contra Gentiles*, I, 30, 33.
[3] Cf. *The Christian Apprehension of God*, pp. 199 ff.

reaches us. The initial "speaking of God" is an analogy,[1] since revelation there takes the form of the event of His self-manifestation. But the speaking of God to us by the words of a prophet is not an analogy. As the name implies, a prophet is one who speaks, actually speaks, for God. Revelation is already in the form of conceptional truth, as it issues from the prophet, and if it is valid in this form for him, it should be so for us also.

The position for which we would argue is that precisely because God's speaking is originally an analogy, affording immediate awareness of Him, it is properly His speaking when it is not an analogy, but in the form of words, which, as we believe, can bring to our minds the relevance of the original divine approach. We must ask what the conceptual truth signifies for the prophet or evangelist who utters them. The concepts and propositions which he gives to the world must be, to himself, consequential articulations of his actual experience of God in act towards him, which experience itself is a living contact rather than conceptual. Concepts applied to things which we have not ourselves met with in actual experience represent to us, as best they can, what we imagine the thing to be. By using them we have "knowledge about" such things, not actual acquaintance. But concepts applied to something we have already met with are of richer significance. They are more than a conceptual representation of the object, because they recall to us not only the object, but our experience of it as our own former experience. They stand in our minds for the whole event of our being affected by an outside reality.

This is particularly true of our thoughts about persons. To represent to ourselves in thought another person whom we have met is to recall our meeting with that person. In the case of the prophet, his conceptual articulations have behind them his direct contact with God, and this is not to be left out of the reckoning in defining the meaning of these articulations. The concepts and propositions which his mind forms articulate not simply God in act towards him, but his own experience of God in act towards him, these being unified inseparably in continuity with each other in the event of revelation. Since this is so, the prophet's conceptual knowledge of God is not reduced, by being conceptual, to the weakness of "knowledge about" God, but retains all the immemediacy of real acquaintance.

The difference between the event itself and its conceptualization as truth is not the difference between revelation and non-revelation, but the difference between past experience and its reproduction in the same mind. Conceptual truth is here revelation

---

[1] As said by P. Tillich and denied by Barth. See *Church Dogmatics*, I, p. 150. E.T.

possessed by mind in the form in which mind retains it, which is the form appropriate to the understanding. The experience of God in act need not be lost in the conceptual reproduction of itself, since the reproduction is more properly a continuation of the effect of the presence of God. When, therefore, we observe, as we must, that the event of God's approach lies behind the truth which articulates it, we do not thereby rob this truth of its status as revelation, but rather point to the circumstance which ensures this status. The form of truth preserves God's actual approach in the prophet's mind because it preserves his own experience of this approach, whence we may conclude that the Word of Truth, at least for the prophet himself, is properly revelation.

As the so-called "truths of revelation" confront ourselves in the written Word, we might of course receive them as mere propositions, static truths about God in His own being. But, if we are to do them justice, we must understand their import, as did those who formed them for us. "God is Love", for example, must be understood by us as conceived by St. John. The evangelist does not thrust it upon us by itself, but explains whence it is derived, preceding it with the statement "and we have known and believed the Love that God hath to us",[1] and in declaring this he forthwith explains its import as the sending of Christ into the world.[2] It is God in active love whom he has known, and of whom he would tell us. The proposition which he gives us, "God is Love", is one whose syntheses are not lateral, on one plane of being, but dimensional. He leads us to conceive that self-relation of the transcendent God to the world which is realized in the descending divine act which took place in Christ. This proposition, like any other of its kind, does have a significance as applied to the nature of God in Himself, declaring as it does the constancy of His attitude toward mankind. But while the nature of God ontologically precedes His acts, the ontological significance of the proposition must follow its "perpendicular" significance from which alone its further meaning can be derived.

To discover the full value of the Word of Truth we must also have regard to the whole process by which it is given us. No truth is achieved by itself, in isolation. It is achieved in and through a continuous process which begins in an actual contact with God, which is at once God's act towards man and also the genuinely human experience of God in act, and ends in the preservation and presentation of this contact to us in the form of truth. The whole process is continuous, and there seems no reason why we should not join ourselves to it as we submit our minds to it. As we receive this Word as the termination of the whole event of God's speaking

---

[1] I John iv. 16. [2] *Op. cit.*, v. 9.

to us through prophet or evangelist, why should not we verily meet with God as so addressing us? The Word of Truth is the declaration to us of the human experience of God; it is comprehensible to us because it is real human experience. If the prophet can meet spiritually with God through divine acts which declare themselves to him for what they are, as God's gracious acts towards him, we also can meet spiritually with God through the whole divine act which now reveals itself to us in the fullness of its grace, the divine act which is God's address to us in giving us the Word of Truth through men chosen for this purpose. "That which we have seen and heard declare we unto you, that ye also may have fellowship with us: and truly our fellowship is with the Father, and with His Son Jesus Christ."[1] It requires indeed the spiritual response of trusting belief on our part for this unified act of God to realize itself as a spiritual contact of ourselves with Him, but given this response by the aid of the Holy Spirit, we would say that the divine act which issues in the Word of Truth can lead us to a spiritual communion with God. In doing so it gives us to know the nature of God Himself in relation to us, not only as manifested in the manifold ways which the word proclaims, but as the God of Grace Who thus savingly relates Himself to our very selves by the giving of His Word. Hence this Word can be revelation in the fullest sense.

We would not, however, demand the full realization of a spiritual communion as necessary for the status of the Word as revelation. It may obviously enough do no more than present to our awareness the fact that God is related to the world as the Word proclaims. But if it does only this it does something for us, and it is God's doing that it does so. The purely objective aspect of its truth is not to be despised, because of the nature of the objectivity, which is not simply a reality in itself but God as He affects our very being. What is proclaimed comes as a warning and a challenge, as well as a promise. The appreciation of it is therefore charged with a moral dynamic by which it tends inevitably to transcend itself as a mere appreciation of fact, and become a truly spiritual relation. When we understand the sheer fact of God's providential care of His own people, which the Word proclaims as extended to ourselves, and when we understand the *de facto* relation of God to one and all through His Will, we can hardly avoid perceiving God as speaking to us personally.

The Old and New Testament stories are certainly not negligible in leading us into spiritual relation with God. We seem to meet Him there in meeting with the facts. Nor is the reality of a spiritual relation dependent on a moral decision of ours. What we decide to

[1] *Op. cit.*, i. 3.

be or do in view of the facts determines what kind of spiritual relation shall obtain between us and God, not whether it shall do so. A saving spiritual relation is not synonymous with a spiritual relation, which occurs whenever the facts are realized to be what they are. We may then claim for the Word as truth that its work in presenting to us the objective aspect of things is an accomplishment in itself, and that it is by being such that it prepares the way for its own further accomplishment of bringing about the kind of spiritual union with God which God desires. We maintain that the purely factual revelation of God's relation to the world has its own divinely appointed object to achieve, in declaring to us the conditions of our existence, and thereby enabling us to live in harmony with the divine Will.

Such is our view of the Word in its present available form. We shall seek to substantiate it further by defending the continuity of the process whereby the Word is given, challenging the grounds upon which this continuity is said to be broken. If the identity of God with His Word holds throughout, from the point of His own initial act to the point of our contact with the Word that issues from it, we shall regard this view as valid. A systematic criticism of the Barthian Theology is not, however, our purpose, and we shall endeavour to confine discussion as far as possible to such points as directly bear on the validity of the Word in the form of truth.

IV

THE BARTHIAN VIEW

I

According to the view expounded in the first volume of *Church Dogmatics*, the Word of God occurs in a threefold form, as Revealed, Written, and Proclaimed. It is insisted that the written Word is not itself revelation. Though distinguished from present proclamation, it is itself the deposit of past proclamation, and therefore stands on the same level with present preaching as the word of a man and not of God, and no man as such can possibly utter the Word of God.[1] The written Word is simply the human witness that revelation has occurred in the past, and thereby also the promise that it may occur again.[2] Revelation is not a "truth", not even the very highest truth. The real Word of God, or revelation, is properly the Word as revealed, which is identified with God's actual speaking in a present address, as an event.

Revelation is thus a spasmodic occurrence, taking place from time to time, whensoever God wills to speak. As a *received* Word of God it is not contingent upon our response to a revelation *already* real, because revelation is not itself a permanent reality. The contingency of the reality, availability and knowability of the Word, lies entirely with God, Who at one time or another realizes revelation and bestows the power to receive it, in one and the same act.[3] Revelation at all times is the *"Dei loquentis persona"*: God speaking; or, alternatively, Jesus Christ.[4] It is to be noted that Barth does speak of the Bible becoming "God's Word" in the event of God's address. "It is to its being in becoming that the tiny word 'is' relates, in the statement that the Bible is God's Word."[5] But it becomes God's Word only in the same sense in which human proclamation is said to become real proclamation. Proclamation is the preaching of the promise of revelation, and proclamation becomes "real" when the promise preached by man becomes a real promise of God to us, which it becomes only through a fresh divine act in addition to the human proclamation. But though it becomes a real promise when used by God, human proclamation never becomes the revelation which is promised.[6]

---

[1] *Church Dogmatics*, I, p. 114 (English translation by Prof. G. T. Thomson).
[2] *Op. cit.*, pp. 125 ff.
[3] *Op. cit.*, Ch. VI, ss. 3 and 4, especially pp. 257 ff.
[4] *Op. cit.*, p. 155.
[5] *Op. cit.*, p. 124.
[6] *Op. cit.*, pp. 74 ff.

So the written Word of the Bible can become a real witness when God chooses to make it so, but it can never, even as thus used by God, become more than a service to the actual "self-Word" of God.[1] Even heard as "God's Word", it only attests past revelation.[2]

The identity of the Bible with revelation is no more than the circumstance that it is somehow used by God to draw attention to the revelation which He wishes to realize towards us. When it is said that the three forms of the Word, as Revealed, Written, and Proclaimed, are all essential to revelation, this does not appear to mean more than that they are all essentially involved in the process by which revelation is given. The written Word has, finally, nothing to do with the content revealed. As a worldly form, neither it nor the worldly events in terms of which it witnesses to God's speaking are fit to express what God has to say to us.[3]

Thus, nowhere in the Bible, not even in the ten commandments, nor in any utterance introduced by the prefix "thus saith the Lord", nor in the words recorded of Jesus Christ, do we have the speaking of God. All we have is human speaking about God's speaking. The recorded word is not God's speaking recorded, but only the sign of it. No systematic clearing up of its content can bring us nearer the reality it indicates by the breadth of a line. The systematic interpretation of it is only the interpretation of a sign.[4] Dogmatics, as the ordered statement of what God has said to the world, in various ways and at various times, is thus impossible. Whereas we would regard dogmatics and preaching on the same level, each being the appreciation, in its own way for its own purpose, of the speaking of God, proclamation is here viewed as only a speaking about God; and dogmatics, at one further remove, as the questioning and revision of how the Church speaks about Him.[5] In dogmatics we are said to know the speaking of God, but to know it only through the prism of our human understanding of it, and all prismatic knowledge or human appropriation of any kind must at once destroy the purity of the real Word, which is discovered to us only by "the light that is perfect in itself, that discovers all in a flash."[6] Thus, preaching can proclaim nothing more than the fact of God's past speaking and the possibility of its repetition, there being no body of truth to be systematically expounded. The Church's faith does not include a trust in the biblical truth about God and the conditions of our existence under Him. It means only that she hopes revelation may be given her.[7]

---

[1] *Op. cit.*, p. 57.
[2] *Op. cit.*, p. 125.
[3] *Op. cit.* See pp. 188 f.
[4] *Op. cit.*, p. 302.
[5] *Op. cit.*, p. 86.
[6] *Op. cit.*, p. 14.
[7] *Op. cit.*; cf. pp. 121, 287.

2

Some of the objections which this theology raises against the conception of revelation as "truth" need not detain us long, since they are directed against this conception understood in a way we are not concerned to defend.

We would not, for instance, maintain that the presentation to our minds of truth as a static, propositional datum represents either the whole of revelation or the whole of its purpose.[1] Revelation is more than this and aims at more than this. What we do maintain is that the giving of truth is revelation, and involved in the accomplishment of its purpose.

Nor would we countenance the atomistic outlook also condemned, which regards every single part of scripture, down to the smallest detail, as a divinely inspired truth, and every statement as of equal finality. In this connection we need only say that we cannot see how such an atomism is necessitated by our acceptance of the written Word as revelation in itself.[2] The Word of God, progressively understood in the spiritual communion of the Church, must itself lead the proof as to what in scripture is, and, what is not, itself; and must declare its own development as the unfolding of the truth. But this it can surely do. If the "*Logos* of God", in the Barthian conception of it, must and can lead the proof as to what it is,[3] the Word of God as scriptural truth can do likewise.[4]

There are also repeated warnings against taking a proposition "*in vacuo*" as revelation. With these we entirely agree. The printed words are not revelation, neither is their verbal form read or heard without their meaning. The Word as recorded contains within itself only the potentiality of becoming a Word to us, which it does only when spiritually received. What matters is not the proposition itself but what it does to our minds, and the Word of truth must be received, not merely as a Word with a meaning, but as God's Word addressed to us as individuals, despite the human channels through which it reaches us. It is indeed doubtful if it was ever preached otherwise, even by the Rev. Thomas Boston, a celebrated champion of the truths of revelation as traditionally understood.[5] But while revelation must come home to us in a living way, whatever its form, this reflection does not

---

[1] See *The Word of God and the Word of Man*, pp. 46, 58, etc.
[2] See Brunner, *The Philosophy of Religion*, p. 34.
[3] *Church Dogmatics*, I, p. 186.
[4] Barth decides that such an influence of a "free Bible" is "improbable"; *Church Dogmatics*, I, pp. 286–302, E. T.
[5] See Boston's Complete Works, especially Vol. IV, pp. 224 ff.

appear relevant to the question whether truth can or cannot be revelation.

There are times when one cannot but suspect that in Barth's thought the necessity of a living reception of revelation is taken as an indication that it must come in one way rather than in another, and that the possibility of truth being received as a dead letter is taken as proof that revelation cannot be offered as truth.[1] A dead letter is certainly not revelation. But it is not truth either. In paying heed to such warnings we are not excluding truth from revelation, as Barth seems to suppose, but excluding what is neither from both.

We thus agree with Brunner when he says that God's Word is not the letter of the Bible as such, but only this letter as understood in the spirit. But we cannot agree that this means that the identity between scriptural Word and God's Word is indirect rather than direct.[2] To say this is to assert that a further act of God, besides the giving of the Word, is required to establish between Himself and His Word a unity which does not exist at all without it. We should say, rather, that although a further divine act is required, it is needed not to create this unity, but to bring to light the unity which already exists. Such we would conceive to be the operation of the Spirit, God acting causally upon men's minds and enlivening them spiritually to perceive that this Word is God's; which is the same thing as to perceive the unity of God with His Word as already real.

On the Barthian view, the scriptural word only bears witness to the possible operation of the Spirit, in which event the unity of God with His Word is achieved, the scriptural word itself being embraced by this unity only as a secondary and instrumental factor which has nothing to do with the content. It seems to us that the scriptural Word, from which we must start as our witness, does not proclaim such a one-sided relation between itself and the Spirit. It certainly bears witness to the outpouring of the Spirit. But it also declares that the Spirit bears witness to the truth of the content which the scriptural Word itself defines to our understanding. The Spirit must, in fact, prove its authenticity by witnessing to the Christ Who came in the flesh,[3] which it cannot do for us now save through witnessing to the truth of the Word through which we know Him. "The Spirit breathes upon the Word, and brings its truth to sight."[4]

What we take to be the real difference between the Barthian

---

[1] See *Church Dogmatics* I, pp. 310–311.
[2] *The Philosophy of Religion*, p. 32.
[3] I John, iv. 1–2.
[4] Hymn 197, R.C.H.

view and our own may be briefly stated thus. The former regards the written Word as instrumentally used by God, not to bring revelation to us, but to bring us to revelation. By itself it can only warn us that we may possibly receive, in another way, a revelation which it itself has no part in expressing. In contrast, we regard the written Word as bringing revelation to us, itself defining what God wishes to say to us; maintaining that scriptural truth is revelation in so far as God speaks to us in, through, and by this form of the Word to which His initial revealing acts have given rise; God's speaking to us in this way being an event unbroken in its continuity. It is the possibility of God's addressing us in this way that the Barthians deny, refusing to admit that the continuity holds. We must defend the continuity, and thereby the validity, of the revelation we receive through it.

3

It would be both tedious and unnecessary to follow in detail the multifarious arguments, or rather expositions, by which the Barthian standpoint is reached and defined. We say expositions in preference to arguments, because the whole position appears to be assumed from the start; and because, while it is progressively expounded by reference to and in contradiction of differing views on each question as it arises, the position seems to be required in its entirety to justify at any point the procedure which leads to its establishment. From the very first it is accepted that the truth of revelation is the freely acting God, Himself and quite alone, in the sense of *"actus purus"*,[1] an event which must become true from time to time, strictly future for us, and from the first accepted that in no other way can the divine freedom and genuineness of revelation be secured.[2] Behind all, at every turn, there appears to be operative an initial pre-view of an absolute discontinuity between God and man; a discontinuity of such a kind as cannot be overcome except in the actual present event of God's self-manifestation.

The Barthian view in its entirety amounts to an expression of this all-determining conviction, and the particular arguments adduced appear as expressions of it in particular regards. As a result, every argument is made to depend on what to us is a false alternative. Objections to other views are cogent only if these are taken to mean what the assumed pre-view of discontinuity allows them to mean. Everything must apparently be either God or not God; either divine or entirely human; either completely tran-

[1] *Church Dogmatics* I, p. 44, E.T.
[2] *Op. cit.*, p. 16.

scendent or completely worldly; and the method of exposition is to show that the purely worldly or human cannot be revelation, and then to assert the entirely transcendent and divine as the only possible alternative. To us this method is fallacious, since the one extreme denied and the other asserted never exhaust the possibilities. But we should not name it so in the hands of its expositors, since for the Barthian mind, owing to its pre-view, there actually are no other possibilities.

This method appears to be, more or less, the general method of exposition. We can see it clearly in the arguments of Dr. W. F. Camfield. It is said that by "immanence" we ought to mean "there is transcendence in the world."[1] This asserts not only the presence of the transcendent God, obviously necessary for revelation, but the utterly transcendent presence of this God, and shuts the door on any discussion as to *how* God is present to the world, as if there were here no problem, as there surely is, relevant to the nature of revelation, admitting of various solutions among which we must choose. It is the manner of God's presence that matters. But there is no question about this manner for the follower of Barth. God must be present in pure transcendence or not at all. This has its inevitable repercussion when we come to deal with the Person of Christ. The humanitarian idea of a purely human, historical personality, Jesus of Nazareth, is cogently and forcibly condemned. It cannot furnish us with revelation. But we nowhere come upon a criticism of such a view as that held by the late Prof. H. R. Mackintosh, that in Christ God puts as much of Himself into humanity as humanity will hold, and in the way in which it will hold Him; a view which permits the revelationary aspect of Christ to be united with and to include His human aspect. The view of Dr. Cairns, who maintained the real divinity of Christ, a difference in kind between Him and the merely human, and, quite consistently, at the same time that the thought and humanity of Christ are revelation, is treated as if it were a humanitarian view, implying a difference of degree only, and as if it intended that revelation were discovered in the purely human.[2]

The possibility of an immanence which renders the human, while still human, such as the purely human could never become but for the influence of the transcendent spirit of God upon it, and the consequent possibility of the revelationary character of the Jesus of Nazareth observed by human eyes, are, apparently, not even to be considered. If not a purely human Jesus, then only a purely transcendent one. A two-nature theory of a Christ's Person is said to be "called for". The Christ after the flesh and the Christ

---

[1] *Revelation and the Holy Spirit*, p. 157; cf. Barth's *Credo*, p. 34.
[2] *Revelation and the Holy Spirit*, pp. 135 ff, 258.

after the spirit belong to two circles, with no substantial, ontological union of the two. The former is not revelation. The *"locale of revelation"* is confined to the "risen and exalted Lord".[1]

When we come to the oft-debated question of the historical influence of Jesus, the procedure is parallel. We find again "the modern conception of a great dynamic, historical personality, radiating spiritual vitality and power," forcibly and indisputably condemned as incapable of transmitting revelation.[2] It cannot unite us to God, but only to man. The opposite extreme is then asserted. The relationship which unites a man with revelation not being a rational, human, causal, immanent one, which belongs to the world only, it must be a divine and transcendent one. The only way of escaping a dynamic human personality, plus its historic effect, is for a relationship already real within God's being (that of the Spirit to the Son) to become in a measure actualized on the field of time, bringing to us a supra-rational consciousness of the transcendent Christ, construed in supra-rational terms.[3] To this a great deal might be said, and it is of the utmost importance to us, since it means that the divine significance of what Jesus said and did cannot be received by the spiritual appreciation of what He said and did. The spiritual appreciation necessary to revelation must mean the appreciation of something else, not of the Jesus of history.[4] The historical events to which the recorded Word draws attention in the first instance being thus removed, the Word is of no direct value. To this we must return, but what we would note now is the absoluteness of the alternative. We never find discussed what may or may not be accomplished by the effects of the divine-human personality of Christ, or of the events of His life, which are more than worldly events because they are the life of Christ, radiating their own unique influence and power through the temporal continuum of human history.

The possibility of our meeting with God in and through what He has accomplished, by His own acts and as His own acts on the plane of event, is not considered. Why not so? It can only be because of the underlying conviction of a discontinuity which makes its consideration superfluous. The thought of T. H. Green,[5] who expounded how a spiritual agency in union with another transforms that other into something it could not be by itself; and does so in such a way that, in the union which is not partly the one and partly the other agency, but altogether both in their union, the character of the secondary agency does not remain in its former uninfluenced state—this thought seems to be quite outside

---

[1] *Op. cit.*, pp. 59–61.   [3] *Op. cit.*, pp. 96–99.
[2] *Op. cit.*, pp. 56 ff, 71 ff.   [4] *Op. cit.*, p. 258.
[5] *Prolegomena to Ethics*, pp. 79 ff, 91 ff.

the Barthian horizon. Barth himself disowns any attempt to explain how God is immanent in Jesus, and in this attitude he is surely justified; but, for Camfield, Christ is definitely partly God and partly man. The divergence of view here is not of moment to us. What is of moment is what is said in common about the causal influence of God in Christ, and of God in revelation in any way, through word or deed. There may be some doubt as to whether in their thought a worldly agency can be taken up by a divine act so as to become itself an agency which counts in the bearing of revelation. There are passages which may be read as implying that this occurs within the present divine act, though, properly, even this is denied. But what is not doubtful is that, even supposing that this occurs in the moment of God's action, once God's presence is withdrawn, the worldly agency cannot in any circumstances retain its divine aspect, its character as used by God. The causal effects which it subsequently has are not the effects of what God made it to be, but only the effects of what the worlldy agency would have been if God had not used it at all.

To express this in Barthian phraseology: the divine "perpendicular", the coming of God to the world, retains its identity as God's act only so long as it remains an absolute perpendicular. It cannot retain this identity beyond the point where it continues as a horizontal through the worldly plane. Within itself, God's Self-Revelation is His own. In respect of its effects, it is not His own. Christ, as a crisis produced upon history, not by history, is God's act: divine, transcendent, and revelation. The effects which flow from His coming to earth are not the effects of God's act. They are effects of a crisis which in giving rise to them has lost its identity as a crisis produced upon history, and become merely a crisis produced by history upon itself.[1]

Here we find a radical difference between the Barthian and the liberal mind. Ask any Barthian whether a worldly agency used by God can produce a subsequent result which is due to God's act, and he will answer "No". Ask any liberal thinker, and he will answer: "Yes". Both will maintain their conviction as with axiomatic certainty. Maintaining opposites as axioms, each appreciates the other's view at times only with difficulty or not at all; at times with pained surprise. Thus, the Barthian readily regards another as holding a humanitarian view, or as attempting to find revelation in the purely historical, when he has no such intention.

To the liberal mind, the Barthian emphasis on the transcendent is not only sound but salutary. In view of certain types of historicism, which invite us to find an impossible revelation of the divine in the purely worldly, it is necessary to affirm that revelation

[1] *Revelation and the Holy Spirit*, p. 96.

transcends the worldly side of the events in which it is realized. But we cannot see that it is necessary, in order to safeguard this transcendence, to refuse either to identify events of history with revelation, or to allow that their divine meaning can be appreciated through study of their record. If we had to begin with mere history, we could not discover transcendence through study of it.

But, on our view, it is not mere history that confronts us as we submit our minds to the prophetic or evangelical records. What confronts us is the prophetic understanding of events as acts of God. Granted an initial immediate awareness of God in His acts, we cannot see what insuperable obstacle stands in the way of revelation reaching us through prophet or evangelist. The whole Barthian position does indeed follow automatically if we accept the negative principle that no act of God can maintain its identity as His in the causal extension of itself through the plane of event and time. For then only a fresh act of God can give us something better than the human and worldly. The historical fellowship of the church which began in the disciples' acquaintance with Christ; its spiritual bond with God through Christ as known by them; its belief and trust in God as the God Who gave Him; its thoughts about God which arise from this bond and express the belief and trust which are part of it; its life and its work, are not then the issue of God's act in Christ. All this is no better than we could have given ourselves, uninspired human thinking and effort. But the negative principle is no more self-evident than its opposite. It depends entirely on presuppositions which we must presently examine.

4

The practical question as to how or when we can obey the divine Will may here be postponed, since the answer to it depends on how or when we can learn of it. What concerns us now is that the negative principle explained above obviously precludes this Will being handed down to us in the form of "truth". We find ourselves justified in accepting the human articulation of God's Will in the form of truth as valid, in so far as such truth is the issue of the reaction of the human mind to a direct meeting with God. But, for Barth, such a reaction is valueless. Nothing that issues from it, whether truth or anything else, is given by God. This position is then strengthened, and indeed rendered apparently impregnable, by the adoption of the view that truth is never the issue of a reaction between ourselves and the real, but always the product of an activity entirely within ourselves.

If truth is of this nature, then obviously enough no Word of

THE BARTHIAN VIEW

God can be a truth; and the conviction that truth definitely is of this nature reveals itself as a basal principle of Barthian thought. In the discussion on the Problem of Dogmatics we find it asked—"Is the truth of revelation—so we must ask by further cross-examination—like other truths in that it may be fixed as ἀλήθεια, *i.e.* as the unveiled state of a hidden characteristic in human thoughts, concepts, and judgments and in the form thus limited and minted, held in preserve, so to speak, quite apart from the event of its becoming revealed as truth?"[1]

We can readily understand why, from this point of view, God's Word must never be conceived as given over to our charge in the form of truth, and why the conceptional repetition of what God has said to this or that man, whether in words of our own coining or in scripture quotations, must be regarded as nothing more than our own work.[2] If truth is something generated from within us, any human articulation of God's Word is fatal to its identity as God's. But we cannot bring ourselves to admit such a view of truth. If truth is not something more than the unveiled state of some propensity within us, there can be no knowledge of anything, let alone of God's Word. To avoid a complete agnosticism, and the facts of life compel us to avoid it, we must at least go the length of acknowledging that truth is a determination of the human mind from without as well as from within; the outcome of a reaction between ourselves and the real, not merely of a human action alone. The possibility of revelationary truth as the outcome of such a reaction with God must be considered.

The nearest Barth comes to examining the possibility of a re-active contact with God is to examine how God's Word can determine a human self-determination.[3] In enquiring how this is possible he analyses and rejects the possibility of an "influx", a special possibility of knowing God's Word given to a religious (or pardoned) man, as a gifted propensity not normally the possession of human beings.[4] It would have the merit of safeguarding the God-givenness of the possibility of knowing God's Word. But its Cartesianism is found to be impossible, and it could never be verified. We could never say with certainty that what any person claimed to be given in this way really was the Word of God. It is not to our purpose to examine the implications of such a view as this. It is an outworn Cartesianism which raises difficulties without achieving results, savouring too much of an "elevation" of man previous to and conditioning his revelationary experience without

---

[1] *Church Dogmatics*, I, pp. 309–310, E.T.
[2] *Op. cit.*, pp. 158–159.
[3] *Op. cit.*, p. 233.
[4] *Op. cit.*, pp. 239–245.

THE WORD AS TRUTH

giving a real contact with God. We would not seek the possibility of knowing God's Word as truth in any specially gifted propensity, but in an actual contact of God with man, from which truth issues as the determination of the human mind directly by the human experience of God. The possibility of a reactive contact is not really examined, while it appears to be so; and in arguing as he does, in assuming that the divine gift of a special propensity for the creation of truth is the only means by which truth could be given by God, Barth appears to be himself guilty of an outworn Cartesianism.

The influence of this Cartesian conviction that truth is generated from within precludes a just estimate of what may ensue from the direct awareness of God. If truth is the unveiled state of a human characteristic, no conceptualization of any kind on the part of the prophet is possible within the event of his experience of God, and no subsequent conceptualization of this experience can allow its essential revelationary character to remain.

The prophet, it is said, can articulate his experience to himself from the outside only, that is, he can characterize it as his past experience of God and so distinguish it from other experiences. But this is only his own "self-witness", not a reproduction of or continuation of the revelation.[1] He cannot articulate its inward aspect. Since the possibility of the prophet's articulation of his experience of God without destroying its true character is essential to our view, being in fact the hinge upon which the divine "perpendicular" turns and continues as a "horizontal", we may quote what is said here at some length.

"When a man recognizes the Word of God . . . there takes place an understanding, a personal sense of being touched, an affirmation, and approval, a concentration of remote times in the present, an obedience, a decision, a standing still before the mystery and a stimulation by its inner life, a founding of the whole man upon this mystery that lies upon his thither side. All that happens and must happen. . . .[2] But not for one moment or in any respect, merely because he is thus in it (the event of God's speaking to him), will he put his confidence in the fact, take his bearings by it, derive from it the measure for understanding the reality in which he stands; he will not reflect upon it at all, but will simply be in it. Not for one moment or in any respect will he dream of coming back on it, holding to it, or building upon it, because he, he, has been in it. . . .[3] If experience of the Word of God is such that it can only have its basis and its certainty outside itself, then in regarding it as real, genuine experience we are bound in fact to take account of its proper, radical

[1] *Op. cit.*, p. 250. [2] *Ibid.*
[3] *Op. cit.*, p. 252.

end, and of the circumstance that here it really involves collapse and death on man's part. . . . Human self-determination even though it actually takes place in acknowledgment of the Word of God, *i.e.* human experience of the Word of God, will, if it is really that, never dream of seeing, contemplating, or regarding itself as determined by the Word of God."[1]

We must concede that, in the very presence of God, conscious, reflective contemplation of the experience as one's own may perhaps be impossible. This would mean that the prophet stood, mentally, at one and the same time, both within the experience, and also outside of it, observing the fact of his being in it; and the presence of the Personal God might well forbid any such concurrent characterization of the experience as definitely his own. We could never determine with any precision either the degree or the manner in which conceptualization may or may not accompany such an experience, and for this reason we cannot definitely assert an immediate articulation of it in the form of truth as taking place within the bounds of the actual experience.

But we would submit that the underlying Cartesian conception of truth which we have noted unduly strengthens and extends the negations which must here be made. If we are not to be ruled by this idea of truth, conceptualization is impossible neither within the actual experience nor subsequently to it, for the operation of the human element from first to last need not be an action, but a reaction. The limitations asserted in the passages quoted are not those of a reaction. As is clearly shown by the repetition of the third personal pronoun, the negations are made on the assumption that what the prophet returns to is his own human experience; this and no more. The reaction is denied rather than analysed. But as a reaction, the presence of human thought, even of articulating thought, need not be so fatal that the experience must involve "collapse and death on man's part". The experience can have its basis and certainty outside of man without this.

And further, although God Himself can never become properly an "object" of thought, only this Cartesian idea of truth can forbid us to say that the human experience of God, the contact and actual meeting with Him, can be an articulate object of thought or expressed as truth. The subsequent articulation of the experience of God is the outcome of the reaction of the prophet to this very experience, not an action of his own undetermined by it. And why should the inwardness of the experience be lost in this subsequent and final articulation? It is admitted that the prophet can articulate his experience from the outside, that he can bear

[1] *Op. cit.*, p. 254.

witness to himself to the fact that he has met with God, and can carry his witness to the world. But how is even this possible, how could he distinguish his experience of God from his other experience, unless in thus characterizing it he somehow preserved its distinctive inward essence as a meeting with God precisely? If the prophet returned to a former expression of his own being, this and no more, we should have to accept every denial of the above quotation. But we cannot accept them, because in returning to his experience of God the prophet is returning to God; and because, moreover, this returning is not merely his own. The prophet articulates his experience in its form as truth because this experience itself includes the reception of the divine command to do so.

5

In this whole treatment, Barth is assuming an anthropology. Anything which man thinks or conceives is the product of himself in isolation, purely and entirely his own.

Here the protests of F. Gogarten are relevant, and seem entirely justified. Gogarten remarks of the Barthian Theology in general that it lacks a "proper anthropology", and that it "speaks one time of a God isolated in and for Himself, over against man, and the next, of man isolated in and for himself, over against God", instead of altogether about God and man in their connection.[1]

With regard to the first point, Barth refuses to discuss an anthropology, or to admit that such a discussion is relevant to the problem of revelation. The refusal is made on the grounds that we must not first determine our doctrine of the nature of man, and thence allow our finding on this question to pre-determine our conception of what the Word of God must be.[2] We may accept this warning without detracting from the validity of Gogarten's protest.

An anthropology in and by itself cannot be the first or the main task of theology. But surely we must discuss the anthropology which the event of revelation itself proclaims and demands for its own explanation. The problem of the anthropology involved in revelation, and the problem of what the Word of God to man is, are one and the same problem viewed from different sides: the problem, namely, as to how God shows Himself to man; or, alternatively, as to how man meets with God.

It is quite true that we must not determine what man's nature is in abstraction from this event, and then determine, in the light of a previous decision about man, what this event must be. But neither must we decide previously what God's speaking must be,

[1] F. Gogarten. Karl Barth's *Dogmatik*, pp. 66, 72; *Church Dogmatics*, I, p. 143.
[2] *Church Dogmatics*, I, pp. 143-149, E.T.

and then understand the event of His actual speaking to man in the light of this other pre-determination.

The one error is as bad as the other, and in fact Barth, in warning us against the first, appears himself to commit both. He comes to the event of revelation with a prejudiced view of the nature of man, according to which man is incapable of reactively receiving God's Word, and on the strength of this pre-determination decides negatively what the actual Word of God to man cannot be: namely, a speaking which remains as a permanent gift.

And, on the other hand, while he insists that the answer to the question "what is the Word of God?" must be evolved prior to and independently of a "proper anthropology", what he does is to determine first what the "Word of God" must be, evolving this prior to and independently of the *actual* speaking of God to man, thereby supporting the same negative conclusions.

This is not, of course, intentional. Barth undoubtedly means to allow God's actual speaking to tell us about itself. But preconceptions appear to adapt the witness to themselves. That the transcendent God can only reveal Himself in complete transcendence is an initial assumption. Neither this nor the assumed anthropology appear to be derivable from the witnesses to revelation. They are alternative expressions of the one all-determining preconception of a radical discontinuity between God and man, which appears to prevent the biblical witnesses from saying freely what they have to say.

With regard to the second point, which is much the same, namely, that God and man are spoken of in isolation from each other, instead of considered together in their relatedness, Barth offers to take up a position towards this objection;[1] but his reply in the following chapter is really a pronouncement that they cannot so be considered.

We read this comment of Gogarten as a legitimate claim that account must be taken of that relatedness of man to God which revelation itself achieves, and to which the witnesses to revelation bear evidence. But the relatedness of which Barth takes account is not this. Instead of a consideration of what the witnesses appear to say he gives us an account of the relatedness which his own conviction of discontinuity permits as conceivable; one which is nothing more than the possibility of man *becoming* related to God by a future divine act. That is, we are given an exposition of the Barthian conclusion on the matter, and the valuation of the biblical witnesses which this conclusion dictates, not the reconsideration of the evidence which is called for.

Here the same thing must be said: that the conviction of a

[1] *Op. cit.*, p. 143.

radical discontinuity precludes the free speech of the biblical witnesses. We must allow the witnesses to speak for themselves. If the events of revelation attested in the Bible proclaim that the prophet does in fact put his confidence in his human experience of God which God has given him, deriving from it his understanding of the reality in which he stands, we must accept their evidence. If they proclaim that God's very Word is lost neither in the prophet's reflective understanding of it nor in his giving it to the world at large, so that we ourselves are related to God by this Word which we are given; and, if their evidence compels us to adopt an anthropology which permits all this to be possible, we must accept their evidence here also. We must do so further in respect of the nature of the reality in which the prophet in revelation finds himself to stand. If there is revealed not only the spiritual communion with God which occurs only from time to time, but in addition a reality in which the whole realm of mankind for ever and inescapably stands, here again we must accept the prophet's witness. We would take our stand on no other.

We must acknowledge that it is humanly impossible to assess any witness with a completely open mind. We can no more hope to escape our preconceptions entirely in appraising the testimony borne to revelation than with any other testimony. But preconceptions may be questioned, and attested revelation may contain some feature which compels us to modify them.

We may therefore call in question the preconceived idea of discontinuity. The ultimate ground upon which this discontinuity is maintained is of course the Fall, which has placed a gulf betwixt God and man. The result of the Fall is viewed in one direction as the anthropological fact that man cannot hear the Word of God; and in another as meaning that an absolute self-presentation of God is required if revelation is to be genuine; a presentation in which God reveals Himself by Himself, and in which the hearing of the Word must be God's also. It is not clear to us whether this last is held as a corollary of the fact of sin, or whether it is an independent preconception. It could be necessary with or without the Fall, but at least it must be treated as a presupposition to be tested by the biblical witnesses.

We shall endeavour to show, first, that the Fall does not necessarily entail such dire consequences as the Barthian Theology supposes; and that neither the effect of sin nor the necessity of an absolute presentation of God need be understood in such a way as to preclude the human hearing of God's Word. We shall then endeavour to evince from attested revelation the special feature which at once contradicts the Barthian presuppositions; and also, as we believe, permits us to accept as God's Word the Word given to us in the written form. This feature is its mediacy.

In studying Aquinas we found it necessary to stress the immediacy of the original experience of God. It is its mediacy which must now be stressed in countering the Barthian denials. The immediacy of revelation secures its God-givenness. If it were purely immediate it could not be conveyed to us through the written Word. But if it is mediately given and received the case is otherwise. What is mediately apprehended must be transferable to a degree by the medium of speech.

The prophets, evangelists, and apostles are akin to ourselves in being men, and by the guidance of their recording words they can direct in our own minds, in terms of our own human thought, some reconstruction at least of what they themselves were given to experience in similar terms. What they experienced by immediate contact must therefore be in a manner transferable as truth to the extent to which their immediate experience is also mediate.

Revelation is obviously mediately given and received in so far as the termination of God's revealing acts occurs within the realm which the human mind can perceive through its own natural, though God-given, endowments, and will still be so though these should require a divine quickening. That is, it is mediate in so far as these acts of God have their term within the cosmos of sin.

Hence we must determine the *locale* of revelation, whether it is without or within this cosmos. If it is within, those who speak for God can give us, if not their own actual experience of God, at least such of it as they were inspired to find relevant for posterity.

In acknowledging the intricacy of the problem as to how an experience admittedly mediate in character could be also immediate, we noted that however difficult the solution, the fact precedes the problem, and that consequently there is small risk in maintaining the fact.

We must now acknowledge that this same problem again confronts us in another form, as it may be asked how an experience necessarily immediate in character can also be mediate. Since the problem is the same: namely, how experience can be both mediate and immediate, the same observation may be made as before. That all experience, however immediate the contact with the real which it affords, not only can be but must be mediate, despite its immediacy, is the factual conviction on which the problem of knowledge stands. For Barth, this is inadmissible in respect of the experience of God. On his presuppositions, any mediacy is fatal, and purely immediate experience must be a possibility. But if mediacy is actually attested, this must surely indicate that it is not fatal, whatever problems it sets us. There may be limits to the degree to which revelation is communicable, but these limits the nature of its own mediacy must partly determine. A true appreciation of this mediacy does appear to justify a different view from the Barthian, and we would seek to maintain in contrast as much as it justifies. We will now turn to the presuppositions.

V

THE PRESUPPOSITIONS

I

According to the Barthian convictions, the Fall means that the *Imago Dei* is destroyed and man thereby cut off from all relation to God, unable to hear the Word of God. "*Homo peccator non capax verbi Domini*": a statement which is only dissolved "in the mystery of the revelation of God the Son."[1] The sin of man has thus caused a much greater separation from God then Aquinas conceived to result from the finitude which precludes acquaintance with the divine essence. Barth allows that we can hear the outward form of God's Word, the worldly form which is the language God must use if He is to address us at all.[2] But this is not to hear God's Word. We are under a double handicap. The whole cosmos which surrounds us, at least this cosmos as we can perceive it, is in a fallen state. Not only do we receive God's Word with our fallen understanding, but we receive it in terms which destroy its true meaning. The place where God's Word is manifest is, objectively no less than subjectively, the cosmos in which sin rules.

The form of the Word of God is therefore that of the cosmos which stands in contradiction to God. It no more has the capacity of revealing God to us than we have the capacity for knowing God in it. God's Word is spoken through the form, the garment of creaturely reality; but this happens in such a way that "through it" means "in spite of it". It is no translucent garment, not a suitable but an unsuitable means for the self-presentation of God, quite incapable of expressing what God has to say to us. It does not correspond to the matter, but contradicts it. It does not unveil it, but veils it. And the veil is thick, too thick for our fallen understanding to pierce through the outer form to the mystery of what lies on the other side of it, the content which is the real Word of God.[3]

Consequently we only have God's Word in its brokenness, form being separated from content. The worldly form without the divine content is not the Word of God, and the divine content without the worldly form is also not the Word of God. To bring the two together is not for man to accomplish. This must take place before there is revelation, in which we must hear the whole

---

[1] See *Church Dogmatics*, I, pp. 252, 466 ff.. E.T.
[2] *Op. cit.*, p. 151.
[3] *Op. cit.*, pp. 188-190.

of God's Word, including form and content, and it can take place only in the mystery of God's actual speaking.[1] But, even in the event of God's actual speaking, form and content are not really united. Even here we only have God's Word in its one-sidedness, which means that in being addressed to us and grasped by us it meets us, not partly veiled and partly unveiled, but either veiled or unveiled. Its veiling may be changed for us into its unveiling, and this change is absolute, so that what we have is either the one or the other.[2] Thus, when it is said that: "God Himself veils Himself and in the very process unveils Himself",[3] we must understand that although this may be a unified act on God's side, it appears to us as two.

The unveiling of God in His veiling, or the presentation to us of the content of revelation in the presentation to us of the worldly form, is not for us the same thing as the veiling of God in His unveiling, or the presentation of the worldly form in the presentation of the real content.[4] And although God veils Himself and unveils Himself in one and the same process, we must not say that God unveils Himself by the veiling, which would necessitate that the worldly form should be capable of revealing God.

It is the divine *acts* of veiling and of unveiling which are united in God's mystery, not the veiling form with the content. Hence the worldly form of the Word of God never becomes the form of the content, even as used by God. The synthesis of form and content[5] is not properly a synthesis of form with content at all, but is their connectedness through the unity of God's act which makes use of the one while it gives us the other. We are led by this act of God from form to content, or from content to form;[6] but no worldly form, nothing which the human mind in its sin can perceive or understand, can ever express the content of the Word of God, nor can it be made fit to do so even by God's own act.

The original reception of revelation must, then, be entirely unmediated by any form of human thought or experience, which cannot carry God's message to us. Only God can reveal Himself, and what He reveals is Himself. Unambiguously stated, this means that pure, unmediated contact with God in His absoluteness is alone sufficient for revelation.

For our own purpose we must, of course, maintain that the worldly form of God's Word is itself revelation. For the view we have maintained requires a direct unity of worldly form with divine content in two senses. We require this unity on the side of God's revealing act, a direct unity of God with His Word: since

---

[1] *Op. cit.*, p. 200.
[2] *Op. cit.*, p. 198.
[3] *Op. cit.*, p. 192.
[4] *Op. cit.*, p. 199.
[5] *Op. cit.*, p. 200.
[6] *Op. cit.*, p. 201.

we have held that revelation is given by God's actual self-relating to the world in a form perceivable by man, which must be a worldly form.

If we are right in this, the perceivable form must be the form of the content, not merely a sign of it. Also, we require a direct unity of the form of human thought, which issues from the reactive meeting of the human mind with God's acts, with the content of meaning which God intends thereby to convey. To maintain this unity of form and content, in both senses, is the same thing as to maintain the mediacy of revelation in both senses. The mediacy of revelation must mean, on the one hand, that it is in and through the medium of perceivable realities and events other than Himself that God chooses to reveal Himself; and, on the other hand, that the forms of human thought and experience, in terms of which God's speaking is received, are adequate to express the meaning it contains.

Ultimately, the question whether this mediacy in either sense is real must be an empirical and practical, not a theoretical, question: since we are dealing with the way in which God has actually spoken. The final answer lies with the witness of the prophets. But before turning to them to determine whether and how far, and with what implications, they declare this mediacy to be a fact, we have now to examine the double basis of the discontinuity supposed to preclude its possibility, namely, the fact of human sin and the consequential necessity of an absolute self-presentation of God.

2

We may begin by asking what the fact of sin necessarily entails. It is a hard doctrine that the *Imago Dei* is totally destroyed. It seems also an impossible one: since if it were true it could not be asserted, for we should be cut off not only from God but from any recognition of our separation from Him; and the question of how His revelation can be given would have neither meaning nor interest for us, which it manifestly has.

Short of such an absolute view, where can we place boundaries to the effects of human sin? We are surely drawing very narrow limits indeed if we say, with Barth, that man is so cut off from God that he can be recalled into relationship by the pure presence of God, but not by an already completed divine act terminating in a worldly form. If his fallen state is such that no Word previously spoken in this way can reach him, why should it not place him outside the reach of grace altogether? If God's present act can restore the relationship, why not His previous act, even though it be to a degree which is only preliminary to a fuller restoration? But in any case the position in which man is said to stand in the Barthian scheme appears an impossible one.

It would be a possible position if we could conceive God's redeeming act as beginning with a psychical and spiritual change wrought in man below the level of consciousness. The effect of the fall being undone by God's present act, a new situation would arise, and with it a new man who previously did not exist at all but now does,[1] who could hear the Word of God. But if the redemptive Word is a spoken Word from the start, given not through the depths of subliminal consciousness but as an appeal to his highest faculties, the position of man is impossible. For if we cannot respond to a Word of God adapted to our understanding in a worldly form, it would seem that we must be not more, but less, amenable to a purely transcendent revelation.

There would appear to be two reasons for extreme care in setting any definite boundaries at all to the situation in which sin has placed us with regard to God's Word.

First, though we may if we choose regard the Fall as a cosmic event, the significance of the individuality of original sin must not be left out of the reckoning. Why should every sinner stand between the same narrow limits? Is it not conceivable that one should be more alive than another to what his environment has to say to him? "Two men looked out from prison bars. The one saw mud, the other stars." As we receive differently the impact of outer reality, some may receive grace through channels that convey nothing to others.

Second, we must beware of setting limits to the grace of God itself. We cannot take upon ourselves to deny generally that anything in the cosmos is devoid of a proffered, revelationary force. Consequently we cannot in any one case deny that the sin which requires to be overcome is adequately met by the grace of God in the perception of what, despite his sin, a man can perceive.

It seems therefore that if we are to begin from the undeniable fact of human sin and argue from it, we can do no more than decide, in an admittedly general way, what sin has made us unable to perceive; and in this way determine, with the same inconclusive generality, where God's redeeming work must begin, where it must meet us if it is to meet us at all. That is, we may, after a fashion, determine the upper limit of the *locale* of revelation. But we can never determine its lower limit, which would be to set bounds to God's grace. This is precisely what Barth seeks to do, to determine the lower limit, and to set it so high that there is difficulty in explaining how revelation is given to us at all.

[1] As is essential according to Barth. See *Church Dogmatics*, I, p. 174, E.T.

THE PRESUPPOSITIONS

The fact of sin limits what God can say to us, because it limits what we can hear. It also determines how God must speak to us, since where and whensoever God's grace meets us, it must meet us in a way adequate to deal with the sin to which it comes. We must at least concede that as a result of sin we cannot, by our own understanding applied either to nature or to the special revelation of God, attain to a knowledge of God Himself in His own essence. Sin must impair our vision of divine realities at least more than the finitude with which it combines. But though it hide from us the divine essence, it need not for this reason prevent us hearing the speaking of God, nor destroy the revelationary quality of the worldly form of His Word, unless it is already determined, independently of the implications of sin, that God's speaking is nothing other than the presentation of His essence.

Finitude and sin need necessitate no more than that God's Word be moralized in its adaptation to the condition of those addressed. To man in his struggle after the fullness of life God's purpose must be revealed as Love, God being thus known as final succour, the Helper, Sustainer, and Refuge of man in his conflict with nature and with himself. To man in his unwillingness to conform with the divine plan, God's purpose must be revealed as final demand, as absolute Will.[1]

Considered in itself, apart from the nature of those to whom it is revealed, God's Will must be a pure indicative. He purposes His own end, and for its sake He now wills towards man that such and such be done by him. For a finite mind devoid of sin this indicative would be sufficient. The knowledge of God's purpose would automatically issue in the doing of God's Will. The saint in his purity need not hear the voice of conscience as an "ought". He need never reflect that its voice is a commanding voice. But, for the sinner, the divine indicative must become a divine imperative,[2] both in its giving and in its receiving. The voice that revealed a purpose to a will opposed to it without being imperative would not be the voice of God. To the sinner who will not, God reveals Himself as He Who says "thou shalt".

It is thus an inescapable implication of sin that it is only through the self-adaptation of God in His Word that we can appreciate what He is and what He wills. Otherwise stated, because of sin, the unity of the form of human thought with the content of the divine message is possible only on the condition that the unity of God with the worldly termination of His acts is realized in a suitable adaptation. Human sin requires the realization of this unity. But it does not disprove its realization. It is sin

[1] See H. H. Farmer, *The World and God*.
[2] Cf. Prof. E. P. Dickie, *Revelation and Response*, p. 64.

that sets the problem. Revelation may show that it is by this very unity that God answers it. What is there to prevent a real unity of God with His adapted Word, and the consequent validity of the human knowledge of God thereby given?

The Barthian scheme can never admit this unity on the divine side. The garments of creaturely reality are discontinuous with God. We must agree that the form of the Word is that of creaturely and fallen man, and agree further that this form is not the form which it would have were it spoken elsewhere than into the fallen cosmos.[1] But why should it require a pure form, in order to maintain its identity as the form of the real Word of God? If the unity is there in the presentation of God to a purified soul, why should it not be there in His presentation to the sinner, even though the form be different? It is surely possible that God should maintain His unity with His own acts whatever these may be, and whatever be the form in which they terminate. God's act must be God's act, even though it terminates inside the cosmos of sin.

Here, we may be permitted to anticipate the evidence of biblical witness, for a moment, and point out that it is within the realm of sin that the termination of God's revealing acts is achieved. And if the *locale* of this worldly form does not prevent its unity with God, what is there to preclude the adequacy of the consequent knowledge of God or His Will? It must be admitted, naturally, that the knowledge of God thus given and received cannot be perfect. So long as God is known through His self-adaptation to our moral and spiritual weakness, He is humanly and morally known; and the moral nature of this knowledge is a sign of noetic weakness as well as a sign of redemptive possibility, since the perfect knowledge of God as He is in Himself must transcend moral categories, if not leave them behind altogether. But we have already argued that to learn of God thus, and also in other ways necessitated by human needs, is to learn truly of God as He is concerned to reveal Himself.

The quality of the human thought involved must of course be affected by sin, and it may even be true that the whole cosmos of sin, including all natural human experience, stands in contradiction to God and is without the capacity to reveal Him. But we have already seen that the distinctiveness of revelation does not consist in the perfection of the materials of thought which God finds in us available for use, but in the synthetic and redemptive use which God makes of this material, whatever its quality. Sin must determine the point whence God begins to lead us to Himself, just as it may fix also the limit of nearness to which we may in our present state be led. Consequently, it must affect also the way in

[1] *Church Dogmatics*, I, p. 189, E.T.

which He chooses to use our thought. But it is to deny God's grace to assert that sin prevents Him making any use of our thought at all. Hence, we conclude that the fact of sin has no relevant consequence beyond necessitating the adaptation of God's Word in ways conducive to its redemptive purpose.

3

Barth will not allow that the moral knowledge of God is any knowledge of Him at all. God known as He Who demands is sharply distinguished from the real knowledge of God, being only the onesidedness of the word in which, if it stands alone, the identity of God with His word is lost. "The Word of God in its veiling—its form—is God's demand upon man. The Word of God in its content—its unveiling—is God's turning to man."[1] This distinction means that God's turning to man, the content of revelation, cannot be realized in His demand upon man, which is its form. But we have seen that the form of demand is the very form which God's turning to man must assume, if it is to unveil the divine nature to the sinner. Sin thus requires a thorough unity of form with content—the very reverse of the second Barthian presupposition which it is seemingly taken to imply. This second presupposition, that a content devoid of worldly form is necessary for revelation, must, then, justify itself; and we may question whether it can do so.

The kind of self-presentation of God which Barth regards as necessary appears very similar to that which Aquinas names as the third form of revelation, the form realizable only after deliverance from the thraldom of sense, namely, the "elevation of the human mind to a perfect insight into things revealed."[2] We cannot, it is true, interpret Barth's view exactly thus. In place of "a perfect insight" we must say "a perfect meeting with God", the perfection of which meeting consists in the entire absence of any operation of worldly or human elements.

Whereas Aquinas looked for freedom from sense in the final state of bliss, Barth looks for a complete freedom from ourselves as well as from all worldly things in the present event of revelation. In the words of F. W. Camfield: "Revelation is God, and God is what we ought to mean by revelation."[3] The supposition that God can be manifested in such an absolute way is fraught with such peculiar difficulties that Barth appears at times to modify his contention. There is a certain dubiety whether the operation

---

[1] *Op. cit.*, p. 208.
[2] *Summa Contra Gentiles*, IV, 1.
[3] *Revelation and the Holy Spirit*, p. 226.

of mediative human elements is permissible at all in the appreciation of revelation, or whether the event is viewed as utterly devoid of these, corresponding to the general dubiety as to whether the causal self-extension of an act of God is or is not possible within the time of its occurrence. But it is the demand for a totally unmediated presentation which at every turn is brought to bear against all assertions of the revelationary quality of the Word in its worldly form, and nothing less than this is properly opposed to the unity of form and content, or consistent with his treatment of the fallen state of man. For all of which reasons we must take this demand as intended in the most absolute sense. If this absolute presentation of God is to be justified as a self-evident *a priori* assumption it must be both possible in itself and consistent with Christian principles. It would appear to be neither.

Such a meeting with God as we are here asked to believe in can be possible only if it represents real human experience, and there is naturally extreme difficulty in explaining how in faith we experience God's Word. How can the Word come home to us at all in our sinful state, if it is to remain pure and undefiled? Formerly Barth had saved the purity of the Word by practically denying that it was a human experience. He held that faith was a vacuum, a void to which the Eternal gave Himself as content. He now finds it necessary to admit that faith is "also" a human experience, with its own proper human attitude which can find expression in definite human thoughts.[1] The giving of the Word is now said to involve human acknowledgment; so that "we must now also lay it down positively that in faith men have real experience of the Word of God, and no *finitum non capax infiniti* and no *peccator non capax verbi domini* should now hinder us from taking this statement seriously with all its consequences."[2] But the need for the conjunction "also" indicates that the real problem is left untouched. If the Word is to remain pure, the real human experience thus allowed for can be no better than a concomitant occurrence. The divine content being given, it might conceivably be consistent with its purity that it should engender a real experience of the fact that it is given, though even this much is doubtful. But how a genuine experience of the pure content itself is possible still remains a problem.

Nor is the difficulty avoided by the explanation offered by Brunner as to what the "giving" of revelation means.[3] The impossibility of having within ourselves standards by which we can

---

[1] See H. R. Mackintosh, *Types of Modern Theology*, p. 284; *Church Dogmatics*, I, p. 208.
[2] *Op. cit.*, p. 272.
[3] *The Philosophy of Religion*, pp. 78–79.

test the meaning or truth of God's Word is here taken to imply that the mind is passive when we accept its meaning as true. It is said that we can neither experience nor understand divine revelation, but only believe it. Faith is the plain answer which we return when God addresses us—I believe and I obey. Thus the assent of faith is our own, but the understanding of faith is not so. But can we thus divorce its assent from its understanding? The reality in which faith believes must necessarily transcend its understanding. But the understanding which faith does have must surely be on the same level as its assent, and both must be ours in proportion as the experience is ours. In the end Brunner concludes that not even the assent is our own. Faith is the miracle that God Himself says "Yes" in us.

It seems, indeed, that the problem of reconciling the absoluteness of God's self-presentation, or the complete purity of His Word, with genuine human experience of it, is insoluble. For we cannot conceive of any human experience other than the mediate. Experience surely means that we ourselves are affected by outside reality in such a way that we ourselves understand it by our own natural forms of apprehension. The experience of faith must mean, on the one hand, that it is we who perceive and understand, we who behold and believe; and, on the other, that what we are able to grasp by our own forms of understanding is the true content of revelation.

So long as the Barthian scheme remains faithful to its separation of the humanly perceivable form from the true content; so long as it holds to God's pure Self-giving as the subject-matter of revelation; and so long as it regards the interpretative processes which constitute human perception as fatal to the genuine character of this subject-matter, the real experience of God's Word seems impossible. If the worldly form and the activity of the human mind are alike condemned, the purity of revelation can only be saved in the original way, by sacrificing the genuineness of our experience of it.

We appear to be driven to Dr. Camfield's exposition as the logical development of these principles, namely, that in faith a supra-rational consciousness is given which is not our own, but the mind of the spirit. We might of course then argue that this supra-rational consciousness, which needs no worldly form of objectification, represents a possible human experience. But it seems scarcely distinguishable from the divinely given consciousness which Albertus Magnus invites us to await in the *"De Adhærendo Deo"*. Albertus here describes how the true experience of God may be attained by progressively emptying the mind of all worldly form, and passing to the contemplation of God *"pure et nude"*, but the expectation was admitted to be a mistaken one, and the experiment confessed a failure. A supernatural consciousness which is definitely human experience while it uses no worldly forms does not seem to be a possibility. To avoid this impossibility we must, then, say that the supra-rational consciousness given by the Holy Spirit is not ours at all, but God's. God in Christ speaks not to us, but to Himself in us.[1] He does not affect our minds save to subdue them, and we ourselves become only the occasion upon which the divine address of God to Himself occurs in a realization on the plane of event of a relation already real within the Godhead. It is God Who presents Himself, and God Who beholds and believes.

Both this explanation and that which Dr. Brunner finds it necessary to offer savour strongly of a spasmodic entheism. The Spirit is constitutive of the essence of the experiencing and believing mind. This may not be according to intention. But any explanation of the regenerated mind which hears God's Word is bound to be entheistic if for any reason we are debarred from allowing full value to the properly creative aspect of the work of the Spirit. If it is we who are to hear the Word, the spirit must be creative rather than constitutive of the "new man" who hears in his still human way.

The Scriptural witness, as we shall see, does allow us to regard the Spirit as the divine dynamic which recreates a mind other than God's with a consciousness verily its own. This interpretation of the Spirit, which is reconcilable with real human hearing of the Word, appears inadmissible to the Barthian, precisely because it is thus reconcilable. It involves properly human activity of thought, and properly human awareness of God in forms of thought suitable to our own nature.

The problem of human experience of God's Word may be considered as that of the old and the new man in faith. Any view which does justice to the creative influence of revelation must face up to the problem of the old and the new, but the Barthian solution of it appears too much like a cutting of the Gordian Knot. The new man who hears the real Word cannot, consistently, be said to be his old human self at all. Indeed, he is said to be entirely new; "one who previously did not exist at all but now does."[2] But regeneration has no meaning unless the new creature is somehow identical and continuous with the old. The old must remain, if it is "we" who hear God's Word. Here, however, the old does not persist with any relevance. It is explained that the capacity for apprehending the Word is lent to man by God, and lent

---

[1] *Revelation and the Holy Spirit*, pp. 72–73.
[2] *Church Dogmatics*, I, p. 174, E.T.

exclusively for use.[1] There takes place, not an adaptation of the Word to man, but an adaptation of man to the Word. "By really apprehending the Word of God in faith he is actually made fit to apprehend it."[2] And it is acknowledged that were this to be denied we could no longer characterize and regard faith as the act and experience of man. But how precisely is it to be affirmed on Barthian principles? It sounds only straightforward Christian teaching to say that by the real apprehension of God's Word we are made fit to apprehend it, but how is this to occur? Is the adaptation of man to precede and condition the apprehension of the Word, or is an initial address of God to the human consciousness on its own lowly level necessary to begin the work of regeneration? The latter alternative cannot be allowed, since it would mean that the thought of sinful man could lay hold on the divine content, and the unity of this content with a worldly form perceivable by him. The former alternative only is consistent with Barthian thought. It signifies an initial operation of grace below the level of consciousness: an elevation; and, consequently, the loss of the identity of the new creature who hears with our sinful selves.

Thus, however we view the problem, the Barthian scheme cannot give us real experience of God. Because of its presupposition that the pure self-Presentation of God is essential to revelation, it is bound to demand that revelation should begin precisely where it must come to an end, namely, where human reception, ceases and only God in His purity remains; and, likewise, that it should end precisely where it can only begin, where the human mind actively receives the self-giving of God. "God" cannot be what we ought to mean by revelation. Some other conception of its subject-matter is required. Only if the subject-matter is such that its worldly form expresses its content, only if what reaches our minds in the form of human thought is what God intends to convey to us, does experience of God's Word seem possible.

4

This second presupposition, then, seems intrinsically impossible. Is it compatible with the kind of fellowship with God in which the Christian faith believes? It does not appear to be so for at least two reasons.

First, the Church is universally defined as a divine-human society, ordained by Christ and sustained by His Spirit. Here it is not truly so. Human acknowledgment and adoration, human effort and personal response, are excluded from the fellowship

[1] *Op. cit.*, p. 272.   [2] *Op. cit.*, p. 273.

itself and must remain external to it. It is undeniable, as Barth insists, that the attitude and thought of true faith must be such as are called forth by God's Word and not that manufactured by ourselves.[1] But this would seem to be the extent of the truth of the principle of the absoluteness of God's self-giving. Through whatsoever events or objectivities God reveals Himself, whatever response there may be from the human side must be engendered by the recognition of God as so revealed. But though the divine initiative is essential, it need not exclude the active appreciation of God by which it calls the human personality to express itself. If this expression is excluded, there is no divine-human fellowship, but only an entirely divine occurrence.

Second, this principle as understood by Barth contains within itself the radical limitation of the whole Barthian standpoint, in that it means that God cannot speak to man in his sin. Just as, with Aquinas, an elevation above the thraldom of sense is required before any vision of God's substance can become a possibility; so, here, an elevation of man above sin is required before he can meet with God. God must first negate the effect of the Fall, subduing all worldliness by a present act, and then speak to the man whom He has thus adapted to His Word. Is this the kind of fellowship which Christianity offers? Does it not rather fly in the face of the whole Christian soteriology? Cannot God speak helpfully and savingly to man in his sin while he still remains in it? The revelation of both Testaments forcibly proclaims that this is precisely what God does, directing our steps through the night of doubt and sorrow, which belongs to the fallen cosmos, by Himself entering this cosmos in the form in which it can receive Him—not by adapting either it or man to Himself, but by means of a Word adapted to our moral and spiritual weakness and by means of the form of a servant.

It is a Barthian conviction that sin is only to be understood in the presence of God. Taken by itself and absolutely, this statement would mean that we cannot say anything at all about sin, either one way or another, outwith the direct divine presence. But the statement must surely be understood within the wider conviction, not specially Barthian, that anything we now say about sin, about its implications, or its power to exclude us from God, must be said in the light of the divine approach to sin. That revelation attests the power of sin to draw us away from God there can be no doubt. But this power of sin is a force and not an absolute result. Nowhere in the whole of attested revelation is there any suggestion that it excludes the entry of divine grace into its own domain.

[1] *Op. cit.*, p. 209.

The view we are considering would, therefore, appear to be not only impossible but also sub-Christian. It cannot, without surrendering its presuppositions, make room for the essential Christian doctrine of *kenosis*. This doctrine implies, not that the fact of sin is negated in order that God may speak, but the very reverse of this: that the requirements of sin are met by the manner of God's speaking, and sin overcome by His power thus to speak. It expresses the power while it expresses the manner of God's grace. *Kenosis* implies the self-adaptation of God. It therefore means that the veiling worldly form is itself the unveiling of God. It means the direct objective and ontological unity of God with the worldly form of His Word which renders possible the direct unity of form with content in the Word as heard and received by man.

The difficulty of how a man can hear the Word of God, of how his human thought and experience of Him can be identical with that which God intends to give him, is not a difficulty to be overcome by a divine avoidance of sin, but one which is overcome by the divine self-adaptation to sin. *Kenosis* means that God reveals Himself as "God-in-relation-to-us", which is the same thing as God in His self-adaptation. Barth, in common with Aquinas, declines to work with this conception. We have found it indispensable, as the only conception which suffices to represent the real subject-matter of revelation. Nothing less divine can spring from God. Nothing more divine can reach to man. The omission or inclusion of this conception in our thinking alters problems and determines certain answers to them.

If we begin by assuming the destruction of the *Imago Dei* and reject this conception, we can only argue as the whole trend of Barthian thought argues: viz., that since what we have in a worldly form cannot be God in His absoluteness, the grace of God must be elsewhere than in the worldly form of His word. But recognizing that what sin necessitates is that God's Word be moralized and otherwise prepared for us in our present state, and including this conception, we may argue in precisely the opposite direction, viz., that since God cannot reveal Himself absolutely, grace is to be looked for in the worldly form which is given us. Can there be any doubt as to the direction in which we ought to argue? Not if we take seriously the kenosis present in all revelation, and especially evident in Jesus Christ the bearer of grace to sin, by which God reaches down to any depth He chooses with the manner of address which that depth requires.

The suitability of the worldly form of His Word to express what God wishes to say to us must depend on what He wishes to say. If it be true that He wills to help us where we now stand, then the worldly form is not only suitable to express His meaning, but is the only form adequate to do so. Adaptation does not hinder, but accomplishes this purpose. The term of God's revelation must be inside, not outside, the fallen cosmos where sin offers its problems, that we may meet with God in and through His revealing acts. Is it not so? "Whither shall I go from Thy Spirit? Or whither shall I flee from Thy presence? If I ascend up into heaven, Thou art there: if I make my bed in hell, behold, Thou art there. If I take the wings of the morning, and dwell in the uttermost parts of the sea; even there shall Thy hand lead me, and Thy right hand shall hold me. If I say, Surely the darkness shall cover me; even the night shall be light about me: Yea, the darkness hideth not from Thee; but the night shineth as the day: the darkness and the light are both alike to Thee."[1]

[1] Ps. cxxxix. 7-12.

VI

THE MEDIACY OF OLD TESTAMENT REVELATION

I

We have argued that the truth contained in the Barthian presuppositions does not preclude the mediate giving and receiving of revelation. We may now turn to biblical sources for positive evidence of such a mediacy as permits the direct unity of God with His Word to persist through the transition from the original experience of it to its rationalization as truth, so that the prophetic utterances are properly the address of God to ourselves.

There is of course an abundance of formal declaration that the prophetic word expresses the very content of the revelation received. Such a prefix as "Thus saith the Lord" attached to a prophet's message shows that he at least intends to produce in the minds of his hearers an impression consonant with the insight given him. This is plainly his intention, and since it is possible only if he has received revelation in terms akin to the forms of thought at the disposal of his hearers we might argue that his very claim to speak for God is sufficient evidence of the mediacy required to make it possible.

But since it is maintained on the Barthian side that "what God said was always quite different from what we may say to ourselves and to others about its content",[1] it could be replied that whatever the prophet's intention, his actual achievement is to give us something other than God's Word. To point to what the prophets say about themselves is obviously insufficient to meet this challenge. But, even though their claim be set aside as insufficient to convince us, either that they heard God's Word or that they had the power to hand on to us what they heard, we are not dependent on their claim alone.[2] Though we cannot enter into the very secrecy of their experience of God, we may examine what their utterances reveal to a degree, the character of the experience which lies behind them.

Here, we must look fundamentally for the mediacy of the divine approach—for the self-adaptation on God's part which renders possible the original mediate apprehension of Him on the part of man, which in turn renders possible the validity and relevance of the Word which we now read. To show that its validity is possible

---

[1] *Church Dogmatics*, I, p. 60, E.T.
[2] Cf. *op. cit.*, p. 248.

is not of course to demonstrate that it is actual. But if the prophetic experience of God is genuinely mediate it will at least be apparent that their claim to give us the real Word of God is a possible claim, and their formal declaration that they do so will be the more convincing. In the New Testament the self-adaptation of God is to be looked for, primarily, in the *kenosis* which took place in Christ. In the Old Testament, with which we start, it is naturally to be looked for in a less complete form. It will be none the less real if realized here in the form of divine acts and as a moral address.

The theophonies which the Old Testament offers to investigation may be classified according to the relative prominence of the natural or corporeal elements involved. We disagree with the statement that there is no Word of God without a physical event.[1] In some instances the physical event is prominent enough, but in others the Word attaches itself only to a past physical event present to the memory of the person addressed; while in others, again, the revelation seems purely spiritual. We may agree, however, that revelation always contains an "upper" and an "under", though not in the way intended by the Barthian use of these terms.[2]

As explained by Barth, this distinction means that everything of a natural or corporeal nature that God uses in revelation belongs to the "under", being entirely subordinate to the "upper", as the spiritual content which no worldly form can express. This understanding of the distinction is acceptable so long as the phrase "natural or corporeal" is intended to indicate physical or other elements as merely such.[3] There must always be a distinction between the elements involved in a divine act, of whatever kind they may be, and the divine act itself, and correspondingly between the valueless perception of these in isolation from their context and the appreciation of the whole act of God.

But this obvious subordination does not seem of much significance. The worldly form of God's Word comprises more than the natural elements which cannot express the content when abstracted from it. It comprises the whole worldly termination of the acts of God as made apparent to the mind of man, and what matters is whether or how the whole worldly form is subordinate to the revelation, and whether or how the appreciation of it in terms of human thought is subordinate to the divinely intended message. Any divine act is in a sense subordinate to the divine attitude which it may only partially express. And on the side of

---

[1] *Op. cit.*, p. 151.
[2] *Ibid.*
[3] Cf. *Church Dogmatics*, I, p. 154, E.T.

human reception we must acknowledge a distinction *within* the content of revelation, in so far as the nature of God-in-relation-to-man, which is properly revealed, is to be distinguished from the pure transcendence which human thought can only acknowledge. But we can find no difference between the worldly form and the content revealed.

It appears that, in so far as God's acts reveal Him, it is by their worldly form that they do so; while it is by means of thought natural to itself that the prophetic mind is enabled to grasp what is thus disclosed. To show this, we turn to three types of theophany; illustrating revelation by portent, by historical event, and by the medium of more or less purely spiritual thought. Before proceeding, we may admit that our inability to conceive of any human experience other than the mediate may so predetermine our interpretation of the experiences attested that we miss the unmediated experience we cannot conceive. But, even so, the presence of mediate experience is sufficient for our purpose.

Portent is obviously sign, pure and simple, the form of its event having nothing whatever to do with the message it is supposed to guarantee; and, if it ever stood alone, exhaustively constituting the worldly form of God's Word, we should then have an instance in which the worldly form performed the subordinate function which Barth attributes to it. But portent is never the real worldly form of God's Word, precisely because it is only a sign. As a survival of pagan religions which, not surprisingly, persists in Old Testament times, it represents the totally unchristian manner or persuasion by sign, without a direct awareness of what is revealed, so forcibly condemned by Christ. Wherefore, at no point in the special approach of God with which we are dealing does portent stand alone. Whenever a sign is used, either it is accompanied by an additional worldly form, the real form of the Word, or else, as in the case of the plumb-line and basket of summer fruit in the vision of Amos, a pre-established connection between sign and meaning is already there in the mind of the person addressed. The symbols named were traditional emblems of judgment and destruction.[1]

An interesting instance of the adaptation of portent is the experience of Elijah after his flight from the persecution of Jezebel.[2] Confronted with the apparent outward triumph of her worship of a Syrian god or force over the policy of righteousness practised by himself and his fellow prophets, he seeks refuge in the solitude of Mount Horeb, the "mountain of the Lord". If Horeb is identical with Mount Sinai this means that Elijah fled

---

[1] Amos vii. 7, viii. 2; Isa. xxviii. 17.
[2] I Kings xix.

to the scene where the God of Righteousness had first made His character definitely known, and where He had covenanted with His people to be their God so long as they respected His law. There follow the three signs of the wind, the earthquake and the fire, and after that the still small voice. Since we are told that God was not in the wind, earthquake, or fire, it is permissible to interpret these as signs only that draw attention to what God had to say. If so, the worldly form of the Word is properly the still small voice. The true medium of revelation is the command to anoint Hazael and Jehu kings over Syria and Israel, and Elisha as prophet in place of himself. There is no difference between "upper" and "under". Elijah accepts the command as God's turning to him, at once the form and the content of the revelation. In and through His immediate presence to the prophet with a decisive remedy for a particular situation, God is revealed as the God who will not desert His prophet in his hour of trial. It is the worldly form in which the divine act issues, the command, that unveils the divine nature. Elijah meets with God through this worldly form of His act, and in terms of it he understands the very nature of the God of Faithfulness.

It is also open to us to regard the three signs as not merely signs but as symbols, turned into symbols by the still small voice and so taken within the revelation and made expressive of its content. Storm, earthquake, and fire naturally enough express the idea of power to the human mind, and may here be intended analogously to express the divine power, signifying that, by the three decisive steps to be taken by Elijah, God would wipe out the Baal-worship of Syria and Israel. If so, they are not only portent, but, though figurative, an extension of the medium by which the prophet conceived God's Will to be expressed. We cannot perceive the cogency of the remark, directed against the possibility of such natural things mediatively expressing the spirituality of the Word, that we must reflect how easily with hearer and even with speaker there begins a slip-back into the sphere of the natural, where the divine meaning is lost and only the movement, pressure, and impact of the natural itself is present to our minds.[1] The natural is used in prophetic expression if and when it draws our minds God-wards, and it would appear to be the natural elements which tend to drop out of reflective contemplation of these expressions, while it is the divine meaning which remains.

[1] *Church Dogmatics*, I, p. 154, E.T.

2

We may now turn to revelation through history. Here we must be clear as to what we take the issue to be. Barth insists that all revelation must be a historical event. But by this he means that the giving of revelation only, not its content, must be so. Revelation must come to a definite person at a definite point in history, making use of a definite physical event as its "under". We may thus speak of a "historical revealedness" of God, in which a relationship between God and man occurs.[1] But, because of its worldliness, we are forbidden to say that any historical event itself can be used by God in constituting this relationship, or that it can be the content revealed. The observation that the term "historical", as applied to such events, cannot have its usual meaning as what a neutral observer might perceive in them is not opposed to our view; but the denial that the movements of history can be used by God to realize His relationship to man or to express His message is so opposed.[2] In contrast, we maintain that they can express the message because they are involved in realizing the relationship.

We find the Barthian position perhaps most directly expressed in the essay of F. W. Camfield. Here, it is explained that the contention is, not that there is no revelation in the historical facts, for example in those of Christ's life, but that these facts do not shine in their own light.[3] Yet we find it contended that when the facts are made to shine by the revelational light of the Holy Spirit, it is something utterly different, something in which they have no part, that is revealed. "In no way is historical event and historical value of any kind to be identified with divine event and divine value. The movements of history, even the greatest and the best, must not be identified with the movements of the Spirit of God."[4]

The reason given for this contention is that no event and no value is a "pure" creation of the spirit. We have already found that this reason is quite insufficient. God may use what is not purely Himself, yet His use of it is His own. We have to show what is denied on the strength of this reason, namely, that specific movements in history are seen by biblical witnesses as divinely wrought, and their historical significance and content seen, not as different from, but as identical with, their divine significance and content. Their spiritual and prophetic perception, we contend, does not mean the perception of some transcendent aspect with which the historical is not concerned, as opposed to the perception of the

---

[1] *Op. cit.*, p. 381.
[2] *Op. cit.*, p. 373.
[3] *Revelation and the Holy Spirit*, p. 284.
[4] *Op. cit.*, p. 220.

historical aspect which does not concern it, but means the perception of what historical events fully are as God's acts, as opposed to the partial perception of them as nothing more than worldly happenings.

We may accept Barth's warning that nothing can be tested with the result that it is identical with God.[1] Applied to our own position, this reminds us that the neutral perception of the historical cannot, by itself, turn into the spiritual and prophetic perception; since no appraisal of events by purely neutral concepts can actually discover their character as wrought by God.

But the truth in this warning does not prevent divinely wrought events being spiritually appreciated from the start, and the spiritual perception of them as acts of God may still be the way of revelation. We may note also that whatever we may be compelled to say about the duality of God's energy in revelation, about the inward operation of the spirit in conjunction with His outward act, or the miracle within in conjunction with the miracle without, cannot affect the relation of worldly form to content in the presented Word which results.

The warning, indeed, would apply equally well to a purely transcendent revelation, were this possible. How could we know, unproblematically, that the transcendent was identical with God? There must always be some reality other than Himself, whether spiritual or physical, in continuity with which God is recognized and met with. But the historical, which combines the physical and the spiritual, seems no more incompatible with an unproblematical acquaintance with God than the purely transcendent would be.

Revelation of any kind requires that God be met with directly. But we say that this can happen in the case of historical event, the prophet being given to meet with event and God in the one, undivided experience. The evidence that it does serve as the medium by which God reveals Himself; that it frequently is the first objectivity pointed out in special revelation; and that in continuity with it the very nature of God is declared and understood, is overwhelming in its richness and abundance. Again and again, events are seen in their fullness as the issue of God's energy in the plane of time. By them God makes Himself to be what He is towards His people. By them He is understood.

It would be hard, indeed, to believe that such a Psalm as the 124th reflects the conviction of God's providential leadership learned in any other way. Actual deliverance lies behind it.

The leading of the people by Moses under God's direction is attested as one indivisible occurrence, at once a continuous

[1] *Church Dogmatics*, I, pp. 513 ff, E.T.

historical event and the very act of God, in which God is directly present to His servant. There can be no doubt that it was so seen by Moses himself. By His guiding in the manner in which He did, always in reference to particular situations and circumstances, God's nature is made known. The liberation from Egypt, the preservation of the race as one, despite the hostilities encountered in and subsequently to the wilderness, and the continued divine interest in this people, despite their recurrent disloyalty, have all something to say about the nature of God. The particular circumstances define precisely what God's act is, and thereby also define His providence and Himself.

In Deut. vii. we find the preservation is not merely the preservation of a race, but of a race numerically insignificant. This worldly circumstance declares the inwardness of God's act in selecting His chosen people. His choice of them is freely His own, with no inducement held out from their side, and no ground for it save His own Will. In Deut. ix. the very unrighteousness and disloyalty of the people, pointed to, not abstractly but concretely (vv. 7, 8, 23), is seen as further revealing the nature of God's care for them. It is not for their righteousness that the land they occupy is given them—no difficulty in pointing to their lack of it. God's act of continuing to regard them despite their disloyalty, His continual recall of them to renewed allegiance, is an act of fidelity to His own covenant, performing the word which He sware unto their fathers (v. 5). In and through His active faithfulness to the faithless, the nature of God as Faithful is expressed by Himself, revealed to man, and understood by man. The fidelity of God to His own covenant is prominent throughout the book. Since it is fidelity, its abiding quality must obviously be apparent in the spiritual perception of any particular event seen as its issue. The historicity of God's individual acts is thus quite sufficient to declare the permanent tie which binds God and His people together. ". . . He is thy life, and the length of thy days" (Deut. xxx. 20).

It may be altogether impossible to show that what God requires of man can be revealed by the medium of concrete events. This, it seems, can only be given in a spiritual address to his moral nature. But the inexorable character of this Will, the unalterable relation of God to His expressed desire, is certainly conveyed, if also conveyed otherwise, in reference to quite concrete events. By the historical rejection of His chosen, God's fidelity is shown to apply to their side of the covenant, as well as to His side of it, and to be a fidelity to a purpose which looks beyond the race chosen in the covenant to be its instrument.

This is naturally most clearly seen at a later date. What is foreseen in Jer. vii. and xi., the inevitable breaking off of the tie between Yahweh and people, as the consequence of unremitting sin, is seen retrospectively to have occurred in the actual captivity of Judah in Jer. xliv., evidently a different writer.[1] The event of the Babylonian captivity is seen as the divine act of dealing with a disloyal instrument. Whether in prospect (vii. 16 and xi. 14 "pray not thou for this people") or in retrospect, in view of the event (xliv. 11 "Behold, I will set my face against you for evil, and to cut off all Judah"), the rejection is seen as of equal finality, comparable with that announced by Amos. The expectation of a remnant to continue as the faithful servant of God is, of course, present to Jeremiah. The captivity is seen as God's way of purging their minds from the false notion of a localized deity who can only be served by ritualistic temple worship at Jerusalem.[2] God is present anywhere to such as seek Him spiritually, and the spiritual worship of the synagogue is everywhere valid. This truth is indeed already declared in the original covenant itself, where the obedience to His voice which God requires is declared sufficient for the maintenance of the tie; but it is in the spiritual perception of the actual exile that the universality and ubiquity of God is now defined and understood.

So, also in Deutero-Isaiah, the event is seen as God's act in dealing with continual rebellion, and as an act of redemptive punishment through which a remnant fit for a new covenant is born. "Behold, I have refined thee, but not with silver; I have chosen thee in the furnace of affliction. I am the Lord thy God which teacheth thee to profit, which leadeth thee by the way that thou shouldest go. O that thou hadst hearkened to my commandments! Then had thy peace been as a river, and thy righteousness as the waves of the sea."[3] For His name's sake, which means for the sake of His purpose, He will turn aside from His anger. God's act is here seen as the act of One who had selected His people, already knowing the evil that was in them, and whose Will to use them for His own ends is therefore not to be turned aside by this evil,[4] but provides its remedy for it in the exile. To the neutral observer the concrete divine acts of preservation and rejection may appear as contradictory opposites. In the prophetic vision, they progressively define and teach, by their interaction, the true character of God's providential purpose. Of historical revelation we may say that not only its giving but its content is a historical reality. Falsely abstracted from the whole, its worldly aspect is not of itself translucent. But as the outcome of controlling divine energy the move-

---

[1] Cf. also Jer. xvi. 11; Isa. xlii. 23.
[2] Cf. Jer. xxix.
[3] Isa. xlviii. 10, 17–18.   [4] Cf. I Sam. xii. 22.

ments of history are expressive of the nature and Will of God. God speaks through them, not in spite of them.[1]

In any revelation, the vision and faith of those whom God calls to His service must not be overlooked. They reveal the divine nature in conjunction with the events which they discern. Revelation through history does not always take the form of an intervention which first turns the course of events, and thereafter produces faith as a result. It is, indeed, questionable whether it ever occurs exactly in this way. Repeated interventions of this kind would not have produced a faith ready to serve, but a complacency content to leave everything to providence.

With the second Isaiah and Jeremiah, as well as other Old Testament leaders, we see things happening in a different order. They show how the faith which trusts in God comes first, determining the course of events and helping to realize the end in which it believes. As Isaiah believed and proclaimed that the afflictions of Israel were a purifying redemption, they would become so for those whose eyes he opened to see this divine purpose in them. It is quite evident also that one main instrument in preserving a spiritual remnant was Jeremiah's belief that the God who sought it could be worshipped spiritually in Babylon without the temple ritual which captivity made impossible. It actually was his advice that prevented the agitation among the exiles from developing into a revolt which would only have ended in their annihilation, and that induced them instead to inaugurate the spiritual worship of the synagogue which produced St. Paul.

It is sometimes thought that God cannot be said to act at all, if our faith must be the means whereby the aim of faith is to be attained. But this suspicion is as false as the contention that faith cannot serve its own object. Faith in a good cause has frequently been a deciding factor in determining the course of history. The faith which God inspires is His gift, and the supreme human instrument of His works. As such, it reveals Him more intimately than any other element in the kind of revelation we call historical, as One whose nature it is to lead us by the way of trust.

3

Since revelation is of God in His relation to man, even the most spiritually given revelation, which makes use of no perceivable act of God in history as the medium by which He is known, must always show some act or condition of man himself in reference to which God is revealed.

The prophet Amos furnishes us with a good example of how the

[1] Cf. *Church Dogmatics*, I, p. 190, E.T.

God of Righteousness can be revealed directly as the abhorrer of actual and particular human evil, with no historical element beyond this evil itself. His condemnation of transgressions is not based upon the previously and specially spoken Word of God, since it is not especially this spoken Word which they violate, but upon the perception that the crimes concerned are so crude and heinous that their condemnation by a special divine Word is superfluous. There are things which man should know instinctively to be sins against God. Amos perceives that there is a relation of God to man eternally established even without the covenant, and thus sees farther into the nature of the covenant-relation itself, as a superstructure of grace erected upon a moral relation already existing. In the quiet of a shepherd's life he perceives the moral order in which he and the whole of mankind are embraced, the divinely ordained continuum which is so constituted that rank evil inevitably separates from God—not so that His voice cannot be heard, since it is heard now through Amos—but so as to destroy the covenanted relationship which ensures the continued use of a people in God's hands and their participation in a final end. "Can two walk together except they be agreed?"[1] No special Word should be required to bring this truth to light. Yet it is given to Amos in a direct address with a direct bidding to proclaim it to a people who are blind.

This Word of God to Amos gives us an example of how the natural moral environment, which surrounds us all and partially constitutes God's abiding relation to the world, contains within itself the power to reveal God's nature, yet may not do so sufficiently for God's purpose. When it is made to do so by a special address, as in this instance, it is in terms of the natural order itself that God is revealed. It is in such terms that the nature of the covenant-relationship is here declared and understood.

4

In the above instance we can only argue to the mediate reception of revelation from the nature of its declared content. But when we turn to the call of Isaiah this is unnecessary. For Isaiah endeavours not only to give us the content but also to describe his experience in which it was given, and in so doing furnishes us with particularly illuminating evidence of the manner in which human ideas and thought grasp the very substance of God's Word.[2] In figurative language he tells how in the year that King Uzziah died he was given a vision of the Lord of Holiness: "high and lifted up"; how the temple kept filling with smoke, the sign

[1] Amos iii. 3.   [2] Isa. vi.

of the presence of something against which the divine purity must of necessity react; how he suddenly perceives that what provokes the divine recoil is not the encroachment of his humanity on the sanctity of the divine presence, but his sin; and how there follows, not death as the reward expected for such an encroachment, but the cleansing of his sin and the call to serve.

The reference to Uzziah is significant. He had dared to enter the sanctuary and offer incense of his own accord, instead of leaving this duty to the consecrated priests; his subsequent leprosy and death being interpreted without hesitation as the punishment for his presumptuous sin against the divine holiness.[1] The idea of God's Holiness had scarcely advanced since the time of David, when Uzziah is said to have put out his hand to steady the ark of the covenant on its journey to the house of Obed-edom, and to have fallen dead as a result.[2] The mention of Uzziah's death can hardly be intended merely to fix the date. It seems clearly to indicate that as Isaiah enters his revelational experience he carries with him this former conception of God's Holiness as a "separateness" of God which it was dangerous for man to violate, and which necessitated even the wearing of protective vestments by the priests in the discharge of their temple duties. In this experience he learns otherwise. God's Holiness is His pardoning goodness to the sinner. It is the pardoning relation of God to the sin of man which is the central subject-matter of this revelation.

In Isaiah's account we may discern two kinds of mediacy.

First, there is the continuity of the new man who hears the Word of God with the old man to whom it is addressed. The vision is presented to the former Isaiah, to whom it is a redeeming revelation from the start; while it is by an Isaiah purged from sin that its full content is finally grasped. The essential subject-matter, God as Forgiver and Purifier, is given to the former Isaiah. God reveals Himself thus, not after, but in the act of, purification. This continuity is also apparent on its conceptual side. Even though the new conception of God's Holiness is new the former conception enters into it. The "separateness" of God which demands reverence remains, while the divine readiness to forgive takes the place of divine aloofness. This latter element is excluded from the new conception, but its very exclusion is part of the revelation. It is the previous idea of God's aloofness which gives to His readiness to forgive the quality and power of contrast, and even of surprise, by which this readiness is so effectively presented.

It is the contrast of new and old, seen together in opposition, which provides the forcibleness of the new. Were this readiness of God not presented in contrast to the previous belief in God's aloof-

---

[1] II Chron. xxvi. 16. [2] II Sam. vi. 6; I Chron. xiii. 9.

ness, it could not be presented at all to this belief, neither to the Isaiah originally addressed nor by him to others who shared it. We should then have to cede that it was an entirely new Isaiah who heard the Word of God, and that what he heard was incommunicable. But since it is so presented, the prophet can and actually does take his stand on the fact that he, with his former understanding, was drawn into this experience, and can and does give its content to the world in the same manner as he received it, namely, in and through this contrast.

We must, of course, recognize that his sin is purged in the process. From this it might indeed be argued that the real revelation is to be confined to what is given thereafter, its content being an incommunicable vision of the Christ, proclaimed only as sign and promise in Chaps. vii., ix., and xi. But, besides what we have said above, we should have expected this content to be at least named in the account given by Isaiah, whereas the only content following the purification is the self-evident divine appeal to carry God's Word to a sinful world. This Isaiah unhesitatingly undertakes to do (not every prophet was unwilling),[1] with no suggestion of its incommunicability. The imperative form of the commission: "Go and tell this people, hear ye indeed but understand not; and see ye indeed but perceive not. Make the heart of this people fat and make their ears heavy, and shut their eyes; lest they see with their eyes and understand with their heart, and convert and be healed", is the grammatical method of stating the necessarily limited outcome of his ministry to an unresponsive community.[2] Only a tenth shall hear. But it is the attitude of men, not the inherent nature of the Word, which determines whether it shall be received.

Second, there is the understanding of the transcendent in terms of the human experience of its impact. The unavoidable prismatic character of human thought, which, according to Barth, necessitates its relegation to the lower sphere of dogmatics, is here observable within the revelational experience. It is not *in vacuo*, but through the impression God makes on Isaiah, the thinker, as the supernatural; on Isaiah, the worshipper, as He to whom reverence is due; and on Isaiah the sinner as He who purifies, that the divine Holiness is understood.[3]

In each shaft of prismatic light the impression is, initially, that of a divine recoil from some human element. In the words of Sir George Adam Smith: "While we recognize the exhaustiveness of

---

[1] See *The Book of Isaiah*, by Sir George Adam Smith, p. 73; cf. Brunner, *The Philosophy of Religion*, p. 163.
[2] *The Book of Isaiah*, I, p. 78 ff.
[3] See *op. cit.*, p. 64.

the series of ideas about the Divine Nature, which develop from the root meaning of holiness, and to express which the word "holy" is variously used throughout the scriptures, we must not, if we are to appreciate the use of the word on this occasion, miss the motive of recoil which starts them all."[1]

The recoil reveals God. To the thinker, it takes the shape of the divine *otherness* from natural things, indefinable save by contrast to them. To the worshipper, God's sanctity impresses itself through the divine recoil from the human irreverence which would approach Him as an equal. To the sinner, His purity impresses itself as the recoil from human impurity. And the recoil reveals God mediately. As the transcendent God is known through His recoil from worldly realities, the nature of these worldly realities is the only clue to the nature of the transcendence which recoils from them. Thus, in so far as this transcendence gives itself to be understood in this way, it is by the mediacy of negative differentiation that it does so. God's transcendence is revealed only in so far as the human act of differentiation is divinely employed to indicate the reality of God as a *beyond* in contrast to some worldly thing or idea about Him.

But the recoil is not the whole of the divine reaction. There is also the redemptive turning not from but to the sinner. "Then flew one of the seraphim unto me, having a glowing stone in his hand, which he had taken with the tongs from off the altar, and he laid it upon my mouth, and said, Lo, this hath touched thy lips; and thine iniquity is taken away, and thy sin purged." As the figurative vision of the seraph's action indicates, the transcendent God remains hidden. Yet He is known positively, as the prophet understands the divine act and attitude towards himself. The divine act of pardon and reconciliation realizes a communion of God with sinner. It is by His entering the realm where He is humanly understood that the impact of God's transcendence makes itself felt, and only so that a communion is realized. Here, God makes Himself to be the active and actual Redeemer of Isaiah's sin.

If it is true that there is no understanding of sin in abstraction from God, it is equally true that there is no understanding of God by the sinner in abstraction from sin. It may seem to us that sin can only be a barrier, but grace turns it into an avenue of the divine approach. The sin of man, far from being an unfit medium for revelation, is the only medium which permits that God should come to sin, as sin requires He should, and therefore the only medium through which the sinner can understand what is of greatest significance for himself in the divine Holiness. Nor is

[1] *Ibid.*

human sin merely the field into which God enters to reveal Himself otherwise than by its help. Sin is anti-God, but sin is shown to be what it is in relation to God, and God is shown to be what He is in relation to sin. Sin is not only a defiance of God, but the defiance of God who forgives it. To forget this would be to miss its worst iniquity. God is not only the Forgiver, but the Forgiver of the sin which defies Him. To forget this would be to miss the greatness of His Grace. Hence the necessity of the confession of sin, with its opposition to God, and the power of such confession to bring to light the Grace which is His. It is as Isaiah sees his own uncleanness in its opposition to God that the fullness of God's Grace is revealed to him.

Thus in the call of Isaiah there seems apparent the mediacy we require. The impact of the transcendent God is received through human experience, and its meaning understood by human thought, since the conscious understanding of the divine act which enters the realm of sin is essentially involved in the reception of the impact. It is the special contribution of this revelation that human sin is no obstacle to the hearing of God's Word, but can be the reverse. Only the particular evil of turning from the Word spoken to sin is such an obstacle. Also, there is the continuity of his former personality with the new Isaiah who is the recipient of this revelation in its fullness. It is the new Isaiah who speaks to us, for he speaks only by right of his certainty that the content of God's Word remain with him as God intends. While it is the new man who speaks, the continuity with the old ensures that the experience in which God's Word is heard is properly a human experience. While the elements of human thought by which the content of revelation is here articulated acquire a new significance in the process, this content is something which these normal elements can be made to articulate. The content received cannot then be such as is altogether beyond the understanding of the common man, nor entirely beyond the capacity of Isaiah's conceptual utterance to convey.

5

We may turn, finally, to Jeremiah to observe what it is that, in his case, and by his own declaration, enables him to speak for God. In asking what gives him the right so to speak we may distinguish between the initial commission, the free act of God in choosing him rather than another as His servant, which is a matter external to the actual work of the prophet, and the inner dynamical relation of the man to God which actually permits him to speak for God.

THE MEDIACY OF OLD TESTAMENT REVELATION

Barth appears to agree that the latter is not entirely explained by the former.[1] Yet it is not evident how, on his view, we can ask with relevance anything beyond the fact of the commission. Proclamation is only the human repetition of God's promise to speak by Himself, and it is true proclamation if and when God, by His own pure and direct causality, turns the worldly hearing of the repeated promise into a real hearing of His promise, and in the same way fulfils the promise by a fresh direct address.[2]

Hence, of the prophet's service, we ought surely to inquire nothing beyond God's decision to use his human words. There is no point, at any rate, in enquiring what enables them to be bearers of the truth, because this they cannot be. Jeremiah, however, not only claims that his proclamation is valid because it speaks the truth itself, but allows us to discern what it is that constitutively qualifies him as the speaker of God's Will. "His right to speak for God rests on the intimacy of his knowledge of the divine will for men. It was his function to measure the actions of men and especially the laws which governed their conduct and their religion, not by their immediate and practical usefulness, not by whether they could appeal to patriotism and national honour, but by their agreement with the only enduring standard, the mind of Yahweh."[3] The Will of God which he knew so intimately was not a new disclosure impossible to others. It was the unchanging will of the divine mind " constantly revealed through all Israel's past for the guidance and help of the people",[4] and now revealed to Jeremiah, as to Amos, especially as the will of God towards the whole of humanity.

Jeremiah thus finds himself to stand, as did Amos, in the immutable moral relation of God to all mankind, and speaks with assurance because he thus stands wittingly. It is this universal moral order by whose standards he is commissioned to judge the nations at large. What qualifies him to speak to the world at large is his naked humanity as contrasted with his Jewish nationality; wherefore he is set apart for his task from before birth.[5] As a man he can speak to man. And, since what he is thus qualified to deliver is the content he is divinely commissioned to deliver, it is his humanity which enables him to perceive this content. Thus not only in the outward but also in the inward direction, it is his humanity which qualifies him as a prophet. It enables him to be in touch with mankind, and also to hear the Word of God which he must proclaim.

[1] *Church Dogmatics*, I, p. 168; cf. p. 64, E.T.
[2] *Op. cit.*, pp. 75 ff.
[3] A. C. Welch, *Jeremiah, his Time and his Work*, p. 35.
[4] *Ibid.*; cf. pp. 41–42.
[5] A. C. Welch, *Jeremiah, his Time and his Work*, p. 41; Jer. i. 5.

THE WORD AS TRUTH

Nor is the humanity which doubly qualifies him sinless. The man God uses remains a sinner. He may fail, upon occasion, to surrender himself to the divine guidance; wherefore his commission confers no irrevocable privilege.[1] But, as is natural for a successor to Isaiah, there is no suggestion that his sinful nature prevents his hearing the divine Word. What the particular sin of failure to surrender himself entirely to God's service interferes with is the accomplishment of the duty of proclaiming the divine will known by his humanity despite its sin. So long as he does surrender himself and so long as he makes clear the difference between good and evil, he has divine assurance that his human words shall be as God's words. "And if thou take forth the precious from the vile, thou shalt be as my mouth."[2] The evidence of Jeremiah thus contradicts completely the claims of the Barthian passage quoted in Chap. IV.[3]

Our question is as to how we are entitled to understand such a statement as this last: "Thou shalt be as my mouth." Do the prophets give us the real Word of God in the spoken truth, or only a sign of the real Word? There appears nothing to prevent the validity of their claim; one, at least, the last examined, giving us the ground and condition upon which he regards himself as faithfully accomplishing his human part of the process by which God verily speaks to us through him.

In the Old Testament, it is by actual self-relation to man in an approach which adapts itself to him by the media of event and moral address that God makes known His Providence, Holiness, and demand upon men. And it is through the media of event and of human idea, which remain event and human idea in the prophetic understanding and use of them, that the approach of God is initially appreciated. The limits to which the divine transcendence thus brings itself into contact with the person directly sought out by God, and the consequent and perhaps narrower limits to which this transcendence can be expressed to us in the Word passed on, or understood by us with its help, must of course be acknowledged. But such would appear to be the limits of the revelation which God intends to give us by such means, rather than to justify a denial of this divine intention. How much the facts and circumstances entitle us to say about the Word passed on to us, we may leave till after we have taken account of the Revelation in Christ.

---

[1] *Op. cit.*, p. 34.
[2] *Op. cit.*, p. 37; Jer. xv. 19.
[3] See Ch. IV, pp. 87–88 (typescript), *Church Dogmatics*, I, p. 254.

VII

HOW IS JESUS REVELATION?

I

The Barthian view identifies all revelation with Jesus Christ, the one and only Word of God. The New Testament certainly declares the revelation in Christ to be paramount. But it need not for this reason compel us to discard the distinctive contribution which the Old Testament claims to give. We must justify such an interpretation of the attested revelation in Christ as does not exclude the genuineness of God's Word given otherwise. We have also to look for the mediacy of the Word which comes through Christ. We shall accomplish both purposes if we can justify the answer we require to the one question: "How is Jesus revelation?" If He is declared to be so transcendently as the one and only Word, we must surrender the validity of the Word as Truth. But if, as we believe, Jesus is revelation in and by His worldliness,[1] and thus as only one, though the supreme determination of God's speaking, the Word as Truth will be relevant in reference to the approach of God in Christ no less than in reference to that of the Old Testament.

We must show that Jesus is revelation in such a way as renders illuminating the verbal truth about Him. With regard to the words which are said to fall from Christ's own lips, we need not argue for the validity of the transition from real experience of revelation to the form of truth. If it is granted that we have the *ipsissima verba*, this transition must here obviously be included within the scope of the divine act; God's presence extending to the utterances of Christ, Who is Prophet, Priest, and King together. If we cannot guarantee the *ipsissima verba*, it will still be apparent that no evangelist would seek to convey to the minds of others, by words which he represents as Christ's own, an impression different from that which he was satisfied Christ Himself intended to convey. The fallible human element cannot of course be denied, and we shall perforce point out our ground for believing that the evangelists faithfully perform their recording task. But it is in any case evident that the evangelists wrote because they were certain that their humanness did not interfere with its satisfactory accomplishment.

From the standpoint that sin prevents our hearing God's Word

[1] This term is used throughout in the Barthian sense as indicating "the garments of creaturely reality."

except in the present event of His speaking, it is a natural, though not an inevitable, advance to the proposition that revelation can be achieved only by the event which took place in Jesus Christ, the approach of God central to the Christian faith. Interpreted as the complete and incomparable downpouring of the inner, the trinitarian reality of God,[1] the coming in Christ naturally presents itself to the Barthian view as alone adequate to overcome sin and achieve God's pure revelation of Himself by Himself.

Thus, in revelation, we are concerned, on this view, with Jesus Christ to come.[2] The years A.D. 1–30 are the era of revelation and disclosure.[3] In the *Credo* it is stated that, strictly speaking, the time of revelation is the forty days after Easter.[4] It is this that the Old Testament proclaims as the word of prophecy, the New Testament as the word of fulfilment; but both as having conclusively, completely, and adequately happened.[5] Revelation is the *Deus dixit*, the "one Word of God within which there can be neither a more nor a less".[6]

We thus arrive at the equation: "God's Word is God's Son"; the converse: "God's Son is God's Word", being obviously true.[7] Maintaining this as a two-way equation, Barth requires much more than the unity which must obtain throughout every Word of God by reason of His presence in every instance. It is not unequivocally stated that the content which actually gets through to us must always be identical in every respect. The observation, that since we have no human awareness corresponding to the divine utterance we can never by restrospect or anticipation fix what the Word of God is, but can only say in what way it is,[8] appears at least to leave room for variations in what may be given to man by the one revelation in Christ. But on God's side the Word is the one Word, with neither a more nor a less. The act of God must always be identical with His act in Christ. Not only is it necessary that God should come forth always with the same fullness of redemptive and reconciling divine energy as is manifested in Christ.

The very particularity of the one determination of divine energy which took place once and for all in the incarnation, the precise individuality of this divine act, must seemingly be repeated in every realization of itself as the one Word to man. The particularity only of the actual years A.D. 1–30, not of the divine act which occurred therein, is said to be dissolved by the divine definition of time which then took place.[9] The equation: "God's

---

[1] *Credo*, p. 26.
[2] *Church Dogmatics*, I, p. 127, E.T.
[3] *Romans*, p. 29.
[4] *Credo*, p. 97.
[5] *Church Dogmatics*, I, p. 130.
[6] *Op. cit.*, p. 136.
[7] *Op. cit.*, p. 156.
[8] *Op. cit.*, p. 149.
[9] *Romans*, p. 29.

Word is God's Son" must be understood to mean not only the qualitative identity of the fullness of divine energy required, but, further, the identity of the result in which the divine energy must always issue; Jesus Christ being the one achievement which God's act accomplishes within itself and presents to man as the content of His Word.

There must, of course, be a certain unity in all speaking of God, whether in point of the manner of approach, or, as is scarcely distinguishable from the manner, in point of what God achieves within His own act. There is a unity in the invariable presence of God, and in the unchanging divine purpose to which everything revealed relates. The Word, moreover, must always be redemptive and reconciling, and to this extent analogous to the approach in Christ. But we cannot see that it is proved either that precisely the same fullness of grace as is manifested in Christ is necessary for every divine approach, or that only what is there accomplished, the one divine act in Christ, can ever be the content. If this last is true, the contingent determinations of the Word in the Old Testament, what God apparently said to His people by the way, as relevant to this or that point of their journey through time, must be excluded as illusory.

Only in so far as the *obiter dicta* are identical with the final Word which God has to say can they properly be His Word. The presupposed view of sin does not itself require that the full Sonship of God be in every Word. Whatever sin may be, it cannot limit the divine energy to one way only of overcoming it. Only the direct claim that Christ is declared to be the one and only revelation can support this contention. The presupposed view of sin does, however, imply that no Word of God, other than Christ, can serve as a preparation for or pedagogue unto Christ. Sin cannot retain any gift from God, so that no preparation of the world for the reception of Christ is possible. Gradual assimilation of divine truth is, then, as impossible for the historically developing world as is growth in grace for the individual. Just as faith must be given in entirety or not at all, so the revelation whose fullness is Christ can only be given at once and complete. Thus the statement in the *Credo*, that only the revealed depths of the mercy that is shown us in the Cross of Christ has power to install the Law as our pedagogue unto Christ,[1] which is logically true of the apprehension of the whole pedagogy of the Law, is, automatically, for Barth, ontologically and historically true also. But, if we are prepared to discard the view of sin which thus makes the limits of logical implication identical with the limits of historical development, this statement may obviously be logically true and yet onto-

[1] *Credo*, p. 43.

logically false. The determination of God's Word as Law may install itself as leader unto Christ without from the start revealing whither it leads.

We have already seen that in the Old Testament the speaking of God can be a real *Deus dixit* in the particular determinations there declared, redemptive, reconciling, and fruitful to the intent which it requires of itself from time to time, even though the fullness of grace to come be neither presented nor perceived. What we must show in this chapter is that the direct witness to Christ does not compel us to understand the revelation in Him in such a way as precludes this—that the attested declaration: "God's Son is God's Word", does not imply its converse to the exclusion of other determinations of the Word; or, alternatively, that there is no ground for the supposed invariable identity of what the self-revealing acts of God accomplish within their own bounds.

If it is natural that, for Barth, the one Word of God should be that spoken in Christ, it is in the end inevitable that only the transcendent Christ should be this one Word. The fallen state of the worldly cosmos must finally determine that Jesus is not revelation in His worldly aspect. It thus becomes difficult to see just how Barth succeeds in retaining either the reality or the uniqueness of the incarnation. It is, of course, intended to preserve its reality. "The incarnation means no apparent and reserved, but a real and complete, descent of God. God actually became what we are, in order actually to exist with us; actually to exist for us, in order, in this becoming and being human, *not* to do what we do—sin; and to *do* what we fail to do—God's, His own, will; and so actually, in our place, in our situation and position, to be a new man. It is not in His eternal majesty—in which He is and remains hidden from us—but as this new *man* and therefore as the Word in the *flesh* that God's Son is God's revelation to us and our reconciliation with God."[1] But the reservation which follows: that "if God and man are not differentiated in Jesus Christ, then God is not free; consequently in the manifestation of Jesus Christ we have not really to do with God's *Revelation*", appears to rob the incarnation of its value.

The necessary ban on worldliness makes it impossible for the humanity or indeed the entire worldly aspect of Jesus to reveal anything through itself as a positive determination of God's Word. Consequently, we cannot regard Dr. Camfield's interpretation of the position as an over-statement, when he declares that the humanity of Christ, being our humanity, must be regarded as something which the divinity disqualifies and negates as such; that the significant thing is not that He lived, but that He died;

[1] *Op. cit.*, p. 66.

HOW IS JESUS REVELATION?

and that it is not in its positiveness but only in its negative and renunciatory aspect, as surrender and self-negation, that the manhood of Jesus which stands out before our view is held up as an example[1] (no distinction being apparently permissible between the positiveness of the merely human will renounced and the positiveness of the obedience of the new humanity which, we would say, emerges as the positive medium by which God's own Will is revealed).

This seems the only consistent Barthian position. The doing of God's Will by Jesus in a human and humanly perceivable way is a worldly phenomenon, and out of the question as revelation. If it is not quite essential to say, with Dr. Camfield, that the *locale* of revelation is the "risen and exalted Lord", at least it must be representatively held that only the transcendent Christ is revelation. The reality of the incarnation is saved in an external way only. God may be present "actually in our place, in our position and situation", and by a real descent; but on this view the immanence of God in the incarnation cannot go beyond the nearness of sheer transcendence. If Christ is the Word *in* the flesh, He still cannot be the Word *through* the flesh. What is said of the miracle of the virgin birth must be said of the whole worldly-aspect of Jesus, namely, that it has no ontic, but only noetic significance; as sign only, as the watch before the door that advertises and draws our attention to the fact that we are here concerned with God's free grace. But how can the incarnation of the Word be real unless the flesh is made to speak the Word of God positively, unless the new manhood in Christ is itself the positive determination of God's Word to us through Him?

We may then ask how, if it is as the transcendent Christ only that Jesus is revelation, the uniqueness of the incarnation can remain. If we must exclude all worldly form from the very Word of God, and the whole Barthian position depends on the circumstance that we must, the Unity of God in His Word can nowhere, not even in Christ, be a Unity declared to us in and through the particular differences of any of its worldly forms. It can only be a Unity declared to us *amidst* these differences which do not enter into the ontology of the very act by which God reveals Himself, or into the meaning of the redemptive Word. Abstraction from the worldly aspect of Jesus Christ is bound to result in the bare Unity of "God speaks". "Jesus Christ" becomes a term which stands as an alternative to this sentence, without adding anything to its meaning. Or, if we like, another name for "the divine initiative which takes place neither in earth nor in heaven, but in God Himself."[2] Or, as Barth again has expressed it: "the Old Testa-

[1] *Revelation and the Holy Spirit*, pp. 53 ff., 271 ff.   [2] *Credo*, p. 48.

ment calls this divine initiative the making known of the name of the Lord. The New Testament names it Jesus Christ."[1] The uniqueness of the Word which comes in Christ is then lost. For the unique significance of the incarnate Word cannot lie in the circumstance that God's free grace and act is truly there; in the fact that "God speaks"; nor in the identity of what is said in any and every revelation. It surely lies in the manner of God's acting and speaking in Christ. As transcendent, Christ may indeed be a distinctive reality of the Godhead, unique without any worldliness. But as Word, as the address and approach of God which gives this transcendence to be understood, the uniqueness of Christ would appear to be nothing, apart from His worldliness.

It is the incarnate Word which is the revelation, and the uniqueness of this must lie in how precisely the free grace of God here determines itself; not in how it determines the position and situation of its manifestation, but in how it determines itself, as distinct from all other possible determinations of the gracious speaking of God. It is not that God acts or speaks, but that He acts and speaks thus; not that God reveals Himself, but that He reveals Himself through the worldly form of a servant; not that God redeems, but that He redeems by this Jesus and the worldly event of His Cross. If there is any point in the remark that all true penitents are children of the Cross, this surely implies not that its worldliness introduces us to a process of reconciliation which omits it, but that the presentation to our minds of this Cross, this worldly event, enters constitutively into the divine reconciling act itself, and essentially so, achieving a reconciliation not otherwise procurable. And, if by this means we are "upward drawn to God", how can we make any division in the divine act which wins us, or say that only part of it is revelation? No division appears possible in the whole reconciling act of God which issues in the event which human eyes can behold, where man may meet with God at the point where divine energy issues on the plane of event. Nor can we divide in two the act by which He reveals His Will through the obedience of the new manhood in Christ. God's approach to us through Christ must be entirely His act, in the free determination of itself from end to end as His act of grace. This approach being unbrokenly God's gracious act, its uniqueness cannot consist only in the locality in which grace appears, but must be the uniqueness of the entire divine act as a precise determination of grace. And the uniqueness of this undivided act of God can be the uniqueness of the incarnation only if the circumstance of incarnation, the worldliness of the Word, is itself the determination of this grace. That is, the Unity of God in His Word must here be declared to us,

[1] *Op. cit.*, p. 45.

not amidst or with, but in, through and by, the worldliness of Jesus. Otherwise the manifestation of Jesus Christ can specially and by itself accomplish nothing for the Word of God, and nothing for His redemptive purpose, which could not conceivably have been accomplished without an incarnation; and it can make no final difference to the world of men whether Jesus Christ ever came in the flesh or not.

We have previously noted that the concept "God speaks" must not be understood in abstraction from God's actual speaking to man. It is true that Barth intends to guard against this danger in proceeding to understand the revelation in Christ by means of the doctrine of the Trinity, it being pointed out that this human document is not directly a statement about revelation, but only indirectly so. The doctrine is the analysis of its root, which is the statement: "God reveals Himself as the Lord",[1] and must always respect its status as the analysis of this root. Yet the analysis at times appears to adapt its root to itself. Christ as understood within this doctrine appears to obscure the real Jesus. We agree that the doctrine of the Trinity is properly a doctrine of revelation. But, as with the Holy Spirit, Jesus Christ must not be initially interpreted as from within it. This is to destroy the freedom of the incarnation as a root of the doctrine, and can scarcely be avoided once the uniqueness of the incarnate Word is gone.

Unless the worldliness of Christ is allowed to stand, determining how God speaks in Him, we have nothing left in our hands to prevent the error of defining God's Sonship by means of our human conception of His Trinitarian speaking, instead of understanding God the Son by means of the Sonship actually achieved towards man in the incarnate Christ.

2

In support of the transcendent view of the revelation in Christ which then results, appeal is made especially to the witnesses of St. John and St. Paul. It will be sufficient if we turn to them and endeavour to show that they do not compel us to interpret Jesus Christ as the one, transcendent Word; but how, on the contrary, they identify the worldliness of Jesus directly with the Word of God, proclaiming this direct identity as the root fact of the Sonship achieved in Christ.

The *locus classicus* for the identification of the Word with the Son is obviously the prologue to the fourth Gospel. It is claimed that, in the trinitarian language here before us, "God's Son" does

[1] *Church Dogmatics*, I, pp. 353 ff, E.T.

not differ from "God's Word".[1] But we may ask in what sense this identity is really intended. There can be no question that St. John here identifies Jesus of Nazareth with the Word, and in the apparent parallel with Gen. i. this involves the further identification of Him with the original creative divine energy which the Old Testament conceived as the "Word" of God. "The Word was made flesh" at least means that the same divine energy which issued in creation now issues also in Jesus Christ as God's perfect Word to man, an identity of energy with energy. We must also recognize from vv. 1 and 2: "In the beginning was the Word, and the Word was with God, and the Word was God. The same was in the beginning with God," especially in conjunction with iii. 13 and viii. 58, that Jesus Christ is proclaimed as somehow timelessly real.

It is the transcendent, pre-existent Christ who comes to earth in the flesh. Thus we must admit not only the identity of the divine energy which appears both in creation and in Jesus, but also a certain identity in what this divine energy achieves within its own operation in both instances, namely, the timelessly real Christ.

But that any further identities are intended is doubtful, and neither of the two which must be admitted appears sufficient for the two-way equation of God's Word with God's Son. Granted that the energizing of the spirit in Jesus Christ is one with the divine energy in creation, there is no evidence that the fullness of grace with which God comes in Christ is required for every approach of God to man. And, granted the reality of the pre-existent Christ Who now comes in the flesh, there is still no ground for the identity of this unique determination of God's being, whether as the timeless Christ or as manifested in the flesh, with the content achieved and presented to man in every speaking of God.

This, the precise identity required by Barth, is precisely the identity which is lacking. It is not necessarily provided in the pre-existent Christ, for the pre-existent Christ, far from being the content of every Word, is not necessarily a Word spoken to man at all. It signifies a reality of the Godhead realized in the beginning, before man is either created or addressed. As such it must mean to us the fullness of God's abiding good-will, which becomes a Word to us only as the Word made flesh. In Christ incarnate, not in the pre-existent Christ, but in the incarnate Word, is the grace and truth of the supreme good-will of God manifested. The Word which was with God in the beginning becomes a real word, an address, by breaking through the transcendence of its own inner

---

[1] *Op. cit.*, pp. 155 ff.

reality and appearing in the flesh. Thus, the eternal Word becomes God's Word to us by becoming the Son. But we cannot say absolutely that God's Word does not differ from God's Son. The prologue entitles us to say only that God's Word becomes God's Son in the fullest expression of the abiding Love of God. It is true that the thought of the prologue begins with the Word and moves in the direction from Word to Son. But the circumstance that thought moves in this direction does not indicate that it begins with the Word as the universal speaking of God and proceeds to assert its absolute identity with the Son. It need indicate only that St. John is following the *ordo essendi* in declaring that the very Word of God is present in Jesus Christ.

The Johannine writings generally are also taken by the Barthian side to vindicate the contention that Jesus is revelation only in His transcendence; not as the Christ after the flesh, but as the Christ after the Spirit. It is said that the aim of the fourth Gospel is, at bottom, nothing other than to present a life of Christ from this point of view, not to show primarily how the Christ after the flesh lived and walked; also that St. John's writings are full of the supra-consciousness by which the Christ after the spirit must be received; the twelfth and thirteenth verses of the prologue to the Gospel, which declare that such as receive Him are born not of blood, nor of the will of the flesh, nor of the will of man, but of God, being taken in proof.[1] But, in fact, the aim both of the Gospel and of the first Epistle would seem to be exactly the reverse of what is here said. While we must be "born of God" to receive the Christ, the spirituality thus required of us does not imply that our understanding of the Word in Him by means of how He lived is excluded.

If we are to accept the prologue as confirming the confinement of God's Word in Christ to a transcendent presentation, we must regard it as a metaphysic of God's speaking, a proclamation that this speaking is accomplished through the identity of the transcendent Son with the transcendent and only possible Word. But to avoid discovering a speculative or metaphysical meaning which St. John does not intend, we must respect the primary purpose of his writing. The real purpose of the Gospel is manifestly not speculative, but practical and religious, with a special end in view at least comparable with that of the first Epistle. Neither Gospel nor Epistle appears to be interested primarily in the relation between the Word and the Son. The essential message of the Epistle is that Jesus of Nazareth is the Son. "Who is he that overcometh the world, but he that believeth that Jesus is the Son of God?" (v. 5). This Jesus Christ is verily He that came by water

[1] *Revelation and the Holy Spirit*, pp. 263 ff.

and blood. The conception "Son of God" appears to be taken for granted; the whole point of this preaching being that we know that the Son of God has now come in this Jesus, who is true God and eternal life (v. 20). God dwelleth, not in whomsoever shall confess the reality of the Son, but in whomsoever shall confess that Jesus is the Son of God (iv. 15).

The Epistle is mainly an emphatic assertion of the complete identity of Jesus Christ with God, as truly the Son of God, proclaimed with the practical religious purpose of refuting the docetism which had begun to separate the saving word of life from the historic Jesus;[1] which is the same thing as to separate the real content of the Word from its worldly form. It thus contains the truth nailed down in the Nicene Creed, that the Very God of Very God does not forfeit His identity as God when incarnate in the humanness of Jesus Christ. There is no interest in the mode of incarnation. The eternal and transcendent and the worldly and historical are simply laid side by side and identified. The opening verse: "That which was from the beginning, which we have heard, which we have seen with our eyes, which we have looked upon, and our hands have handled, of the Word of life" (i. 1), declares in brief this identity which, together with its implications for the religious life, it is the practical aim of the Epistle to lay before us.

The aim of the Gospel appears to be parallel to the Epistle, namely, to proclaim with all possible emphasis the identity of Jesus of Nazareth with the Son and Word of God. To an appreciable extent it is a book of signs that the historic Jesus, whom men saw, heard, and remembered, is indeed the Christ, or Son. There is the sign of the turning the water into wine in Cana, which the evangelist distinctly declares to be the beginning of signs by which Jesus manifested His glory to His disciples and won their allegiance (ii. 11). There follows the sign by John the Baptist, and thereafter the sign successfully given to the Samaritan woman and the Samaritans (iv. 39), in which the identity of Jesus with the Messiah is declared by Himself, as it is frequently elsewhere; and the equally successful sign to the nobleman of Capernaum (iv. 53). Other incidents, such as that of the loaves and fishes (vi. 14); the raising of Lazarus (xi. 27); the appearance to Thomas after the resurrection; and the miraculous draught of fishes transferred by St. John from before it to after it, are subordinated to the purpose of manifesting this identity. The sign of the healing of the impotent man at the pool of Bethesda is portrayed as directly challenging the unbelieving Jews, who resent the verbal claim of Jesus which follows and elucidates it, namely, that of His

[1] See H. R. Mackintosh, *The Person of Jesus Christ*, p. 120.

HOW IS JESUS REVELATION?

identity with the Son (v. 18). The gift of sight to the blind beggar at the pool of Siloam is a sign to the Pharisees in particular. Everything possible is subordinated to this same purpose; even parable, such as that of the Bread of Life (vi. 30 ff.) and that of the Good Shepherd (x. 6 ff.), being adapted to pressing the claim of Jesus against the distrust in His Sonship which repeatedly appears, and which is given an entire chapter to itself (vii.).

The prologue appears to render to the Gospel a service similar to that derived by the Epistle from its opening verses. The Gospel as a whole declaring the identity of the worldly Jesus with the Son, the prologue announces concisely the identity of the worldly Jesus with Son and Word together. The use of the term "Word", or *Logos*, is ideally suited to express this identity, whether to the Jews or in opposition to the heresy which denied it. In the time of Christ, according to Dr. Marcus Dods, the "Word of the Lord" had become the current designation by which Jewish teachers denoted the manifested Yahweh.[1] The use of the term would therefore signify for any Jew the real manifestation of God in Jesus. A word is also something which is not itself without the speaker. To quote Dr. Dods again, it is "capable of being used by no one besides, but by ourselves only."[2]

To describe Jesus Christ as the "Word" of God is thus a very serviceable way of expressing the direct presence of God in Him in contrast to the Gnostic conception of an intermediary. The *Logos* of Philo was carefully separated from God. Neither was it God, nor could it enter the process of history.[3] The same term in St. John's hands denotes that whether as creative Word or as the Word of manifestation in the historical process, God Himself is verily present in Jesus Christ. The suitability of the term in its Christian interpretation to refute its own implications in the Gnostic setting is sufficient explanation of its use. Its choice need imply no transcendent metaphysic of God's speaking in Christ. The subject of the Gospel being not the *Logos*, nor yet the Word of God in general, but the divine Person of Jesus Christ, we must not turn to the conception of the *Logos*, nor to any preconceived idea of the Word, in order to understand how Jesus is Word; but, on the contrary, must turn to Jesus of Nazareth to understand how the Word is here spoken.[4]

Thus, the prologue declares the reality of the incarnation, without seeking to explain its mode any more than the Epistle. The truth and grace of God break through their transcendent reality

---

[1] *The Gospel of St. John*, Vol. I, p. 4.
[2] *Ibid.*, p. 7.
[3] *The Person of Jesus Christ*, p. 116.
[4] *Op. cit.*, pp. 115-118.

and are declared to us in and through the historic Jesus. What God has to say to us and do for us in Jesus Christ meets us here in the worldly form. While the worldly life of Jesus is portrayed as a series of signs that He is the Christ, the signs are not external to what they signify. The kind of persuasion by sign which seeks to dispense with a direct meeting with what is revealed is quite foreign to the faith which Jesus taught. It is in fact entirely out of harmony with the manner of God's special approach to the world at all times. The demand to be so persuaded asks too little of God, and is dead to the gracious nearness of His approach. For this reason it is as forcibly condemned by Christ in St. John's Gospel as in the synoptics. "Except ye see signs and wonders, ye will not believe" (iv. 48).[1] It is a spiritual impossibility for any one to be led thus to faith in Jesus as the Son of God. What He looked for was that men should directly behold the Grace and Truth of God in His visible Person, the gracious act of God in His words and deeds. And St. John testifies that men actually were led to meet with God in Christ by the simplest human deeds of Jesus, and so to confess Him as the Son of God (e.g. Nathanael ii. 49). According to his witness, the works that Jesus did declared Him. The appeal to believe on Him because of the works; or, failing this, at least to believe the works themselves as the works of God, is put into the mouth of Jesus Himself (v. 36, x. 25, xiv. 11, x. 38). St. John lays before us "the things which Jesus did" (xxi. 25), leaving them to do their appointed work for us. "These are written, that ye might believe that Jesus is the Christ, the Son of God: and that believing ye might have life through his name" (xx. 31).

Above all things, Christ evinces His own trust in God the Father as the heart and soul of the Christian life in which He inspires His followers to share. The active manhood of Jesus is the expression of this trust, and, according to St. John, the explanation of God's Will for us on earth. "This is my commandment, That ye love one another, as I have loved you" (xv. 12). If He had said only, "That ye love one another", He would have given the world merely something of its own, the recommendation of the love which it already knew; to the Jews of his own time not indeed a very lovely gift. But the commandment is: "As I have loved you." "For I have given you an example, that ye should do as I have done to you" (xiii. 15). The circumstance that this is a commandment is doubly significant. Rationalized as such in the words of Jesus Himself, we may take it that it is God's Will that is here rationalized and given us. And as a commandment addressed to men, the content is something to be used and reproduced by men in their own human sphere, the divine interest being in the life

---

[1] Cf. Matt. xii. 39; xvi. 1; Mark viii. 11; Luke xi. 29, etc.

lived in that sphere. Its content cannot then be something to be understood in transcendent, supra-rational terms, but must be understood in terms of the sphere of new human life to which it refers. The incarnate Word thus brings to us God's Will for our present life, expressed in the form of command and defined for our natural understanding in the faith and life of the historic Jesus.

Thus, St. John's testimony is diametrically opposed to the Barthian view. On the one hand, it contains nothing which confines the real Word to the Word in Christ. And, on the other hand, it is the special intention of Prologue, Gospel, and first Epistle as well to declare that the Word in Christ is revelation, precisely in the way that is denied, by the worldly and humanly perceivable aspect of Jesus. The question we are here concerned with is expressed by Barth in a threefold way. "Can the Incarnation of the Word according to the conception of the Bible witnesses mean that the existence of the man Jesus of Nazareth might have been as it were in itself, in its own power and continuity, the revealing Word of God? Is the *humanitas Christi* as such the revelation? Does Jesus Christ's Sonship to God mean that God's revealing has now, so to speak, passed over to the existing of the man Jesus of Nazareth, and the latter has now become identical with the former?"[1] To this it may now be said that St. John's witness at least confirms the reply that the question in each of its three forms of expression is a false one, falsified by the preconception of sin which assumes beforehand that a worldly form must be merely that and no more. It is not a question of the humanity of Jesus being "in itself" revelation, nor of God's revealing "passing over" to the existence of a "man" of Nazareth. According to St. John, the unique and transcendent inner relation between Father and Son, the inner oneness, is revealed by the veiling form, by what Jesus of Nazareth was and did before human eyes; including the positive obedience of His manhood as the revelation of God's Will for men on earth.

3

St. John, along with St. Paul, certainly does stress the spirituality of revelation, and we would not deny that if we are to do justice to the spiritual reception of God's message which the New Testament writers require, we must describe God's revealing act as two-fold. It is by the inward working of the spirit, repeatedly testified while it remains beyond any explanatory statement, that we are given to meet with the transcendent God declared and revealed by the manifold worldly forms of His Word outwardly

[1] *Church Dogmatics*, I, p. 371, E.T.

presented to us. It is this that we believe the spirituality of the Word properly means. We meet with God's act coming to us in what is outwardly presented, not with a mere objective presentation. The content is all that then confronts us, God's transcendence not being otherwise revealed. According to the Barthian conviction, the spirituality of the Word means that we are brought to meet directly with the transcendence, understood in transcendent terms supplied by the Holy Spirit, whose operation means the complete removal of what is presented from the worldly to the transcendent sphere. The main witness here is St. Paul, and there is no reason to suppose that St. John differs from him. We must ask what St. Paul means by spirituality.

The spirituality which St. Paul preaches is not concerned solely with the hearing of God's Word. No New Testament writer is so concerned with the conflict between the Spirit and the flesh. To be carnally minded is death; but to be spiritually minded is life and peace.[1] Spirituality means, on the one hand, the subjection of the flesh with its dangers for the Christian life. At the same time it also means that the things of God must be spiritually discerned, taught by the spirit of God which searches the deep things of God,[2] and which is scarcely distinguishable from the Spirit of Christ or the Indwelling Christ through Whom St. Paul could do all things. It is not the natural man, to whom they are foolishness, but he that is spiritual (v. 14), who receiveth the things of the Spirit of God.

Spirituality, according to St. Paul, thus means at once the subjection of the flesh and the subjection of worldly wisdom in understanding the whole truth of God and Christ, these two aspects being given fairly equal prominence. The inclusion of both aspects within its scope at once suggests that spirituality has a practical and *total* meaning, denoting in all references not a metaphysic of hearing God's Word, but the whole life of faith engendered in us, as contrasted with that which is unconverted and natural. The Spirit enables us to receive the Word, but this does not mean the exclusion of the worldly Jesus from the Word that is heard. It is true that no other writer gives such prominence to the transcendent Christ, the risen and exalted Lord; and texts are admittedly not wanting which, taken by themselves, appear to substantiate the general interpretation that it is the transcendent Christ, understood in terms supplied by the Holy Spirit, Who is the real revelation. Yet the "Christ after the flesh" and the "Christ after the Spirit" are not opposed. The risen Christ would have no meaning unless identified with, and to some extent at least explained by, the Jesus who was seen and remembered. Nor

[1] Rom. viii. 6. [2] I Cor. ii. 10.

HOW IS JESUS REVELATION?

does the subjection of worldliness within ourselves, whether the subjection of the flesh or the subjection of worldly wisdom to the mind of the Spirit, imply the subjection of the worldliness in Christ as the object of faith. The spiritual discernment of the Christ after the flesh is still a possibility.

The transcendent Christ is certainly prominent in St. Paul, but there are reasons for this prominence. It has been held as a defect and a loss that he was never a companion of the earthly Jesus. Had he been so, he would doubtless have given more prominence to the historic Jesus. Yet neither had other evangelists the benefit of such companionship, who give us plainly the story of His life. How much St. Paul learnt of the detailed life of Jesus is problematical, but at any rate his temperament was apparently such as did not require any wealth of detail or incident to define to himself the truth which for others detail must articulate.[1] His philosophical temperament is thus a subsidiary reason, but the circumstance of his conversion gives a fairly sufficient explanation of his love for the transcendent. It was the sudden revelation that Jesus of Nazareth was indeed risen, and exalted, the very Christ and the Son of God, that changed Saul the persecutor into Paul the servant of Jesus Christ; and we can readily understand how he could do no other than live spiritually thereafter in the world of transcendent reality. But if he had no need of worldly detail, neither does he appear, as Canon B. H. Streeter remarks, to have felt any need to think out an intellectually watertight theory of the relation of Christ to the supreme and only God.[2] And, as a missionary first and all the time, it could hardly have been his purpose to give to the infant and struggling churches to which he wrote any such systematic theory, nor yet to give them a metaphysic of the working of God's Spirit in revelation. It seems scarcely credible that he intended to define a relation already real within the God-head, that of the Spirit to the Son, realizing itself in our minds as revelation by a projection of itself into the field of time, or that he intended to equate the revelation in Christ therewith. Sufficient for St. Paul that Christ is the power of God unto salvation, with no definite limitation of the way in which He is this power.

There is no passage which appears deliberately to limit this power to the transcendent Christ, and the many passages appealed to at one time or another to support the contention that revelation is so limited, particularly those on spirituality, would all seem at least capable of a simpler interpretation. Thus the opening chapters of I Corinthians, whose theme is that the Spirit of God

[1] See Hastings' *Dictionary of Christ and the Gospels*, II, pp. 887–888.
[2] See *The God Who Speaks*, p. 131.

alone can enable us to perceive the truth in Jesus Christ which the natural man cannot perceive, do not appear to have such a far-reaching implication. St. Paul had tried at Athens the experiment of attempting to persuade a pagan community that the religious expectation of its own natural and worldly wisdom would find the revelation of the Cross and Resurrection to be the truth which satisfied that expectation.[1] The experiment was failure. The Cross and Resurrection were foolishness to those who judged them by the wisdom of the world. But the distinction here drawn, between the spirituality which sees the truth and the natural wisdom which does not see it, appears to be drawn not within the circle of such as deem themselves to belong to the household of faith, but between the whole body of believers and those who reject the Christ. The natural man is unspiritual not because he finds the events of the life, death, and resurrection of Christ to be themselves revelation, nor because he forms his conception of God and the world by what these events have to say, but because he is not influenced at all by these events; because he turns from them as foolishness, and remains determined in mind by the preconceptions of his worldly wisdom. Faith in Jesus Christ cannot stand on worldly wisdom. It can only stand in the power of God. Wherefore St. Paul now determines to dispense with all attempts to persuade by appeal to worldly wisdom, and to allow the Cross of Christ to do its own work, preaching Jesus Christ and Him crucified, directly and only.[2] Only the spirit of God can help us to see what Christ and His Cross verily are, the act and approach of God to us.

But it is worldly wisdom that St. Paul dispenses with, not the worldly side of Jesus. There is surely no point in contrasting the spiritual discernment of Jesus Christ with the natural discernment which fails to see what He is, unless the spiritual discernment begins with the same thing as confronts the natural man. The attention of the spiritual and of the unspiritual is drawn to the same manifestation, the result being the perception of different things by different minds. The natural man sees a bare event which is just that and no more. The spiritual man meets with the act of God towards himself in what he sees. The work of the Spirit is thus to bestow the power of receiving the whole event of God's coming and speaking in Jesus Christ; corresponding to what we found to be the prophetic appreciation of the events of the Old Testament, the appreciation of them in their wholeness as God's acts; not as occurrences complete within themselves, this prophetic vision being the similar gift of the same Spirit of God.

The significant statement in II Cor. v. 16: "Though we have

[1] Acts xviii. 23 ff. [2] I Cor. ii. 1–5.

known Christ after the flesh, yet now henceforth know we Him no more", is said in the *Church Dogmatics* (p. 168) to denote "a definite relationship of the historical understanding with Jesus Christ", but a relationship which did not contain within itself the power by which men came to recognize Jesus Christ as the Son of God. The "κατά σάρκα" is here interpreted as especially describing the understanding, rather than as referring, as in the work on *Romans* (pp. 103, 160), to the "Christ after the flesh"; but, for Barth, it may consistently describe both, since, on his view, the worldly understanding can only be concerned with the worldliness of Jesus. There may be some doubt as to what exactly St. Paul intends, but the point that matters for us now is whether or in what way the relation between our understanding and the "Christ-after-the-flesh" presented to it is here declared to be insufficient. The bare presentation of the worldly Jesus to the understanding is certainly insufficient according to St. Paul. But, considering that the chapter is deeply concerned with the eternal reality of God, our true spiritual home, and of Christ our eternal judge; and with the continual spiritual presence of God to the believer throughout his burdensome life on earth, it may be doubted whether, in this quotation, St. Paul intends to say more than that we are not cut off from fellowship with Jesus Christ now that His presence in the flesh is withdrawn. Christ was once known in the flesh, not by St. Paul but by former Christians for whom he speaks, and who form, together with St. Paul and his contemporaries, one continuous body of believers to which the "we" refers. Now He is known spiritually, yet it is the same Jesus Christ Who is known. There is no evidence upon which to alter our view that what is given by the Spirit, and would otherwise be lacking in the relation of our understanding to the historic and worldly Jesus, is not the capacity of the Christ-after-the-flesh to direct our minds in apprehending the truth which God intends us to understand, but our capacity to be persuaded that what we here behold is God's Son, and that what is thus taught is the truth.

4

I Cor. xii. 3 declares plainly what the vital function of the Spirit is: "Wherefore I give you to understand, that no man speaking by the Spirit of God calleth Jesus accursed; and that no man can say that Jesus is the Lord, but by the Holy Ghost." Here, again, the division is the broad one between disbelievers and believers. This division was made real by the Spirit for St. Paul himself. Does not the division as here expressed point us straight back to his own conversion? The word "accursed", "ἀνάθεμα", indicates precisely what Jesus of Nazareth was to the unconverted Saul, and to every orthodox Jew. Saul the Jew already believed in a Christ, but as a Jew who so believed he despised the man of Nazareth, regarding His claim to be the Son and Word of God as sheer blasphemy. His conversion by the Spirit meant, not that he now believed on the Christ, but that he now believed that this Jesus was the Christ and Son.

The significance of Jesus Christ as the Son and Word of God cannot be other than what Saul the Jew failed to see, and what Paul now sees by the Spirit, namely, the direct identity of the worldly and historic Nazarene with God's Son and Word. For it was the worldliness, the human aspect and the worldly life, and the humiliation of the Cross, which the Jew despised; the latter, though not the former, continuing to savour of humiliation even after the conversion. Saul had already believed on the power of God unto salvation, but not that this humility was itself this power. Could his conversion have meant only that the power of God unto salvation is now seen to be realized and fulfilled; that his Jewish hopes are justified, the man of Nazareth announcing and signifying that they are so? For this is what the Word in Christ would amount to, if his worldliness were only a sign, instead of the very Word and way of redemption. The conversion must have meant not only that these hopes were fulfilled and justified, but that they were fulfilled here in this way in Jesus Christ, fulfilled by the difference between the transcendent self-realization of God's promised redemption and its actual realization in the man of Nazareth. Saul had served God, not in abstraction from belief in Christ, but in abstraction from trust that the worldly and historical Jesus was the divine power of God which he knew the Christ to be. He now serves God, not in the belief that the worldly Jesus has by divine appointment, as sign, introduced him to the reality of the prophetic promise, but in the belief that the Nazarene is Himself the realization of this promise. If we remove the worldliness from the very revelation in Christ, what have we left that Saul did not believe?

It is in so far as the Word in Jesus Christ is *not* pure transcendence that Christianity differs from Judæism, and St. Paul from Saul. To subordinate this worldliness is not to take account of, but to omit the central theme of St. Paul's teaching on, the Spirit, which declares the same identity so strongly emphasized by St. John; that of the historically known Jesus with the Christ and Son of God. In reality, St. Paul seems about the last person to whom to appeal in support of the separation of the worldly side of Jesus from the very Word and revelation of God.

But, indeed, nowhere in the New Testament, except perhaps at

HOW IS JESUS REVELATION?

one point, is the Spirit which reveals Jesus Christ represented as revealing Him in pure transcendence.[1] The possible exception is the transfiguration, witnessed only by the three disciples who seem to have been in particularly close fellowship with our Lord. Yet even here it is not sheer divinity that is revealed. As is evident from Mark and Matthew, it is along with His approaching sacrifice that the Sonship of Jesus is now made more thoroughly apparent. The dimensional depth of Him whom they knew as companion and leader, and now as vicarious sufferer, is indeed manifested in a manner we can scarcely discuss—a manner which the evangelists indicate as reminiscent of the Baptism. But if the transfiguration presents problems beyond solution, transcendence here breaks through in a way outwith the general trend of the Old and New Testaments; and if the synoptics had meant that only this was revelation, they would surely have said so. They do not suggest this, and the main concern of them all is to give us straightforwardly the whole story of the coming of Jesus Christ to earth and leave it to do its work of grace.

Nowhere in real life are fact and what we may term worldly values found separately. What life shows us is fact revealing value.[2] In a sense the Incarnation is the divine recognition of the circumstance that religious value, or religious truth, or God Himself, can only be given to humanity in conjunction with events or manifestations which we meet with in our own human realm. The truth of God the Father is revealed by Christ the Son; by His life and work; by His sympathy with men and women in the burdens, sorrows, and testing experiences of life. So do we learn of the nature of God, as Love and as Will. It seems rather like calling unclean what God hath cleansed if we refuse to Him the power of declaring what He is towards us by means of the homeliness of human life. As remarked by B. H. Streeter: "Christ made possible an attitude which we may call 'friendship' between God and man; in a sense He brought God down from heaven to earth. And, ever since, there have been theologians who have tried to push Him back again."[3]

At times the New Testament does give the impression of sublime transcendence separated from the life of the world; this both with regard to the divine approach and with regard to the Christian life we are thereby called to live. For this reason it has been said, not without point, that the New Testament would be a dangerous book if used by itself without the Old. The Old Testament never made the mistake of separating religion from life. It could not

---

[1] Cf. *Revelation and the Holy Spirit*, p. 89.
[2] See A. E. Taylor, *The Faith of a Moralist*, I, p. 55 ff.
[3] *The God Who Speaks*, p. 119.

separate its religious life from the world, for the revelation which directed and defined it was received in and through the life of man and nation. The Old Testament will not permit us to forget this, and we must be prepared not only to look to Jesus Christ to understand the import of the earlier revelation, but also to look to the Old Testament, as did Christ Himself, to understand aright the revelation in Him. What God does for us in Christ is the completion of what He does for us through the former Word; and the Old Testament may remind us that, neither on the side of its giving nor on the side of its receiving; neither on the side of God's approach, nor on that of our hearing, is God's Word to man to be removed from the sphere of the problems of human life and the struggle of humanity after the good.

VIII

THE IMPLICATIONS OF MEDIACY

I

We may now see how we stand as to the answer which attested revelation permits us to give to the question whether the Word passed on to us as Truth is revelation in itself. When the question is raised whether or not we possess the real Word in the written Word, we cannot agree with Barth's dictum that the issue is between those who regard the Spirit as a *datum* and those who regard It as a *dandum*.[1] The issue can only be so stated if the whole Barthian position is already conceded. For, while we must maintain the unity of the written Word with the Spirit, we need not reduce the Spirit to an inert *datum*, in order to do so, unless it is already agreed to be impossible that any such Word should be unified with the free active Spirit of God. Since the Spirit is God in act, It must always be a *dandum*, both in the outward act of God's Self-presentation in the actual event of revelation, and in Its inward operation, which is necessary both for the original recipient at the time of this event and subsequently also for others, in order to show the revelation in its true light. But though we are agreed that the Spirit is always a *dandum*, the real issue would appear to remain: namely, whether the required unity of the free, active Spirit of God with the content, received through and expressed by the written Word, is or is not possible.

We agree that the present inward operation of the Spirit is necessary for the Unity of God with His Word, but not that a fresh outward operation, or self-presentation of God, is essential. This God may give. But we differ from the Barthians in maintaining that God's Word may be His without it. Once the actual approach of God is achieved by the twofold divine act of outward presentation and inward visitation, can it or can it not leave to the world Truth which is God's own gift? Here Barth says: "No". Others who are just as insistent on the spirituality of the Word say: "Yes". Otherwise stated, the question is whether the truth which issues from the reactive contacts of men with God is properly the effect of the divine approach. If it is such an effect, the truth is then the final term of God's outward approach to us, in which the distinction between mere sign and real content becomes untenable. The Word of Truth cannot be so much as a sign except by revealing itself as properly the address of the Personal God to us through

[1] See *The Holy Ghost and the Christian Life*, pp. 11 ff.

His original approach. If the deposited truth is properly such an effect, it is always with us, permanently there to do its appointed work to whatever extent the inward working of the Spirit may determine.

Barth evidently regards the Spirit as either specially given or else completely absent. But is it not rather a permanent *dandum*, if always a *dandum*, as God's active power always present to us in some degree? Moral experience tells us that we are less than the conditions of our existence permit us to be if there is not sustained within us a life of aspiration. Such a "life" cannot be given or withheld from time to time. Though it may come to light only at intervals, it is surely the permanent and distinguishing feature of human creaturehood that conscience proclaims can be ours. If the presence of the divine is needed to sustain it, this presence must be inward as well as outward. God presents Himself outwardly in and through the opportunities of endeavour which life offers, thus providing the moral person with a religious aim. But there must also be sufficient spirituality within us to permit our response to this outward presence of God. In so far as our created nature retains its divinely given spirituality, this response is already possible. If we accept the survival of the *Imago*, we are already supposing that the free, active Spirit of God is permanently effective. The Spirit which is a *dandum* in its creative operation is then effectively with us always. Nor can it be disproved by any logical or human consideration that the Spirit is also given as a continuous and present *dandum*, effective in proportion as it discovers minds responsive to God's approach in the special Word.

Thus, the indispensability of the Spirit need not worry us. We need not regard It as either completely given or completely withheld. Nor need we regard the capacity to hear God's Word as one which we possess either entirely or not at all. Indeed, it seems impossible to regard anything about God's Self-giving or what issues from it, either the giving of the Spirit, the hearing of the Word, faith, or the Christian life, as ever completely realized or unrealized. If we do justice to the dynamic aspects of the giving and receiving of revelation, we must allow that it is real though incomplete. We can only speak of the work which the Spirit does, not of Itself as present or absent; and consequently also only of the degree to which it is possible to hear God's Word, whether given otherwise or through the extension to us of the direct address formerly given to another.

When it is questioned whether it is God's real Word that comes to us in this latter way, to begin with, we cannot lightly pass over the scriptural witness of both Testaments, both direct and circumstantial, which affirms that it does so. We cannot ignore the

THE IMPLICATIONS OF MEDIACY

circumstance that when God speaks in the Old Testament He is by no means exclusively interested in the spiritual welfare of the prophet directly addressed. On the contrary, the prophet is a servant, and the divine interest extends primarily to the welfare and progress of the nation indirectly addressed through him. Prophet and people alike, and indeed all who hear God's Word, find their spiritual well-being in their inclusion in a service to what lies beyond, while it includes, themselves. Were God interested in the prophet alone we might then find it possible to admit that what God said to him could only be known by him in the actual event of its utterance. But since the divine interest is in the Word passed on, whatever we may think of the epistemological problems involved, God Himself at least is satisfied with the direct Unity of Himself with His Word as heard by those to whom it is not directly addressed. What is present to the contemporaries of the prophet and lacking to us is not the direct address of God, which Barth regards as paramount, but the immediacy of their own environment and the prophet's personality. Such mediative factors do not give an unmediated presence of God. Wherefore we and these contemporaries stand on an equal footing in point of indirectness of address; and if we must say that God's Word reaches them as He intends, unified with His Personality as He intends, we may surely say this also with regard to ourselves.

The New Testament likewise furnishes us with a sufficiency of evidence that the Unity of God with His Word in Christ is preserved in its self-extension through the fellowship of the Church. In the seventeenth chapter of his Gospel, St. John gives us an insight into the close filial relation of the Son to the Father. Jesus has sent out His followers to preach the Word, and as He sees that their labour is not in vain He perceives that His own labours are not in vain. Their success is the success of His own work. Accordingly, He gives thanks to the Father that His mission to the world is accomplished through His followers. "I have finished the work which Thou gavest me to do (v. 4). As Thou hast sent me into the world, even so have I also sent them into the world (v. 18). For I have given unto them the words which Thou gavest me; and they have received them (v. 8), and they have kept Thy Word" (v. 6). And the Word which they have kept and successfully delivered is the Word of Truth. "Sanctify them through Thy truth: Thy Word is truth" (v. 17).

There could not be a more thoroughgoing declaration that God's Word in Christ is continued through His human followers, and carried to the world as the Word of Truth. The circumstance that St. John is bold enough to declare so much as the private thought of Christ in a prayer of thanksgiving need not indicate that it is only the opinion of the evangelist. St. John must have been unshakably convinced that this was the mind of Christ. It is not too much to say that St. John's conviction that the revelation in Christ is validly continued in this way must be included in his conception of the Sonship of Jesus. The same conviction is expressed further in the opening verses of the first Epistle. "That which we have seen and heard declare we unto you, that ye also may have fellowship with us, and truly our fellowship is with the Father, and with his Son Jesus Christ" (I John i. 3).

It is remarked in the *Church Dogmatics* (I, p. 514) that this announcement is "the indication of a reality, the possibility of which in the New Testament is by no means to be taken for granted", and the words of St. Paul in II Cor. iii. 5 are cited in proof, "not that we are sufficient of ourselves to think anything as of ourselves". But if we complete the quotation, which continues: "but our sufficiency is of God", we may perceive that, in harmony with the context, St. Paul does not mean that he or others do not have this sufficiency. On the contrary, he appears emphatically to declare that the followers of Christ do have it, but have it of God and not of themselves; wherefore their sufficiency is real. Every preaching may not be true, of which obvious possibility St. Paul warns us. Nor is the spiritual hearing of the Word more than a possibility. But the preaching of the Word by the evangelists is an actuality which definitely is to be taken for granted. The Word is heard only within the fellowship of the Church, but this fellowship is not to be looked for or awaited as a pre-condition separately generated. Rather is it the counterpart of, and generated by, the declaration of the Word. The New Testament conception of God's Sonship in Christ includes the faith that the fellowship He began on earth can declare the Word, thereby continually recreating itself as the living fellowship of the Church; wherefore the Church itself may be truly described as the "extension of the Incarnation".[1]

2

We have argued that it is the Barthian philosophy, with its presupposed view of man and sin, and its view of truth as a product of an inner propensity of the human mind, that is properly responsible for the decision that any such self-extension of the original approach of God is impossible. But only the attested nature of this approach can ultimately determine whether or not it can accomplish what it apparently claims for itself. The approach of God being two-fold, the evidence is also two-fold. There is evidence of how the Spirit works inwardly and the

[1] See *The Person of Christ*, L. W. Grensted, Ch. III, p. 56.

evidence of the nature of the outward presentation. We have sought to show that in both instances the scriptural evidence supports our view. The scriptural description of how the Spirit works is, as it is bound to be, mystical. Hence the hearing of the Word must take place *by* God's mystery. But this does not justify the oft-repeated Barthian statement that it takes place only *in* God's mystery, as an event from time to time achieved by God. The mystery is that of the inner nature of God's act. But the result of His spiritual energizing, the understanding of His Word, need not be entirely mystical.

If the Barthian interpretation were correct, there ought to be no witness which declares that the gift of the Spirit is the understanding in faith of what the outward, worldly form of God's approach reveals Him to be; whereas with the all-important revelation in Jesus Christ this would seem to be precisely what the witness does say. The Spirit enables the natural man to perceive that Jesus of Nazareth is the Son of God. If, however, it is claimed that the witness may also be understood to imply that what the inward Spirit empowers us to receive is the present approach of God, devoid of all worldly form, of which possibility the spiritual understanding of the worldly form only warns us, the attested nature of the outward presentation must then be the deciding evidence. Accordingly, we have sought to show the mediacy of God's Self-presentation, and to find in this mediacy the circumstance which will explain how the truth which ensues is still His Word, unified with Himself. In both Testaments it is the worldly form which God takes to Himself that is declared to be the revelation. The veiling form is itself the unveiling of God. The worldly form which veils and unveils is both form and content, between which no difference is attested.

The mediate approach of God which the Scriptures declare appears to us the only approach possible. So long as God is God and man is human, revelation can be only mediately achieved, and only mediately received. It is by bringing Himself into touch with the hopes and aspirations, the fears, weakness, and sin of human life that God makes Himself known. While the evidence is that this approach reveals God to us as He desires, the Barthian anthropology inevitably dictates that it cannot do so. As God reveals Himself in answer to the spiritual questionings of the human soul, He is known by human thought; which, according to Barth, can result only in the experience which man can give to himself of the fallen cosmos in which he lives. Against this we have argued that the mediate experience afforded is properly experience of God.

How direct, though mediate, experience of anything at all is possible is a problem in itself. But, as this general problem does not specially concern us, we have done no more than point out that the conviction of the fact precedes the problem, remaining a primary conviction despite all difficulties. What concerns us is the specifically theological problem of how mediate experience of *God* can be direct and real. Here, also, since attested revelation is the final authority about itself, the attested conviction that God is directly, though humanly, known must appear to many sufficient evidence that so much is possible. In any case, revelation must be allowed to explain the human awareness of God which is its own accomplishment. The human awareness of God is the divine act of self-revelation viewed from the side of man. It is God's act, in which He takes upon Himself the task of so presenting Himself that we can understand Him humanly. The very event of revelation is already the adaptation of divine things to our understanding. Sin, the root of all the difficulties Barth has raised, is no fatal obstacle to our hearing the Word, since it is especially to human sin that God savingly relates Himself. We thus feel justified in accepting the mediate experience of God as a divinely grounded possibility and an attested actuality. It remains to determine what we believe it entitled us to say about the Word passed on to ourselves in the form of truth.

3

The Written Word is revelation if it is unified with God as the informative effect of His approach to man. It must be so unified before it can be a divine gift. It must also enable us to understand God as He intends. This last involves two distinguishable conditions which must be fulfilled; in that the Word must give us a true appreciation both of the objective and of the subjective aspect of revelation. First, the understanding which it gives us of God's relation to the world must be that understanding which He intends us to receive thereby, since otherwise it is not the true content which reaches our minds. Second, this content must be recognized and received as Subjective. It must be received as the address of the Personal God, as God's Word precisely, according to all that is implied in the sentence "God speaks". If these two conditions are fulfilled we have the real Word of God, which cannot demand more for itself than that we should hear its true meaning as God's address. The two conditions cannot really be separated, as each implies the other. Only as Subjective is the character of God's relation to us made known. Only in approaching us in some way definable by the understanding can God address us at all.

THE IMPLICATIONS OF MEDIACY

But for the purpose of discussion we may focus on one condition at a time.

To take the preliminary condition first, the deposited truth itself may be seen to retain the required unity with God when we do justice to the manner of His approach and adopt the anthropology which this implies and warrants. Neither prophet nor evangelist leaves the sphere of his own life while God speaks to him. Both remain in this natural sphere, in which God finds them by joining Himself to it. The sphere in which they then find themselves to stand is not a different one, but is the natural sphere enriched by God's Self-union with it. The very terms of God's Self-union with human life, as divine Love which abides towards it, as divine Demand which requires of it, and in both of these as the divine Power which controls it, imply that the new richness brought into human life is henceforth a permanent element in man's natural environment. It cannot but be understood as such by those addressed. The experience of God at the moment of address is the experience of the permanent conditions of their existence. A prophet might, of course, fail to live thereafter in his divinely enriched environment, but that is not to say he cannot succeed in so doing. If sin and the general limitations of human nature do not prevent his hearing the Word of God, there is no reason why they need prevent his divinely given experience from continuing with him. Nor is there any reason to suppose that what he has to tell us is only the product of an inner propensity of his own nature. If the significance of his experience of God remains with him, he can tell the world what it signifies for the world.

Thus the recorded Word is unified with God, and, as the completed outward speaking of God to us, we may call it revelation in itself, if we so desire. But it is the truth received, the understanding of God which our minds finally possess through contact with the recorded truth, which ultimately matters. Recorded truth of any kind is both instrumental and mediative in the service it renders us. As an expression in words it is instrumental, causing the receiving mind to act, so that its thinking is its own. But words are also mediative, directing the mind in its contemplations, so that the possession of reality by mind is properly the outcome of the reaction of the mind to the deposited truth. We have to ask whether the mediate speaking of God can retain its unity with Himself through this final reaction, which might destroy it, so as to give us the true content. With regard to its objective aspect, it will not be denied that, where the ordinary events of life are concerned, the experience of one is communicable to another by the instrumental mediacy of words, at least to the extent to which experience is mediate. Experience means that we are affected by outside reality, and in so far as different persons have a common human nature each can understand how another is affected by an agency whose effect on himself he knows directly. The precise individuality of the experience of one may not be communicable, but where all the elements which go to make up that experience are common property, the synthetic guidance of words can communicate its nature, and thus can introduce others to the way in which reality has affected him, and thereby introduce them to reality in a new way for them.

We can thus say at least that the Word as Truth can introduce us to the several objectivities, the worldly events and ideas, in continuity with which God is known in revelation. But this by itself is obviously insufficient. It is not only the objectivities, which may be known in the unspiritual interpretation of the Word, but the content of revelation: God as known in and through them, the new richness of the prophet's environment, which must be communicated. And we must also recognize that as the prophet himself acquires an enriched humanity in his awareness of God, so likewise is our nature changed in appreciating the enriched environment to which he introduces us. Yet this does not seem impossible. The familiar process of teaching by the mediacy of words designedly and successfully uses what we do know to bring us face to face with what we did not know before, and we are proportionately enriched within our own being in the process. How it is so may be ultimately inexplicable, as a living, conscious organism is inexplicable; but to be capable of learning in this way, with corresponding inner development, is obviously enough the nature of the living human mind. To be capable of learning of God through the appreciation of familiar worldly events unified with Him by Himself, and to be spiritually enriched in the process, ought, at least, to be natural to the creaturehood which takes its origin from Him, provided of course that this creaturehood is not totally destroyed. It is true that such events unspiritually perceived cannot imply God as their source. But a living mind in contact with reality is not confined to the logical implications of a partial apprehension of it. If the limitations of human nature do not prevent the person originally addressed from understanding God as revealed through the worldly and familiar, neither need they prevent ourselves from understanding Him through the record of His approach in this way.

As we receive God's Word through the bequest of prophet or evangelist we cannot indeed acquire the very individuality of their experience of God. But to acquire this would be superfluous. What must be sacrificed here must be sacrificed in consequence of the very success of revelation given in this way. If revelation gets through to us it must give us, ultimately, not the individuality of God's address to another, the nature of which only need be understood, but the individuality of His address to ourselves. We neither can nor need understand God precisely as did the person directly addressed. For one thing, it is not the same divine impact as that out of which the prophet's thought was born, though it is still a divine impact, into reaction with which we bring ourselves when we read the words he leaves us. Isaiah met with the direct impact of God's universal goodness particularized towards his own sin. The impact of God's goodness which reaches us through the written Word includes, while it comes through, that of itself upon Isaiah, and as it reaches us it is the impact of this universal goodness particularized towards our own sin. Besides, an exactly equivalent understanding would be possible only if we could bring into reaction with this impact a life experience and a sin exactly equivalent to that of Isaiah, whereas we can only bring our own. Consequently what we severally learn of God the Forgiver cannot be identical with what the prophet learnt. But we must not ask mediate revelation to accomplish what no revelation at all need accomplish. Through whatever channels it reaches us, whether through a human medium or otherwise, the Word of God must find us at our own level, and what we receive from it must be limited by our own being and condition. For God's Word to reach us through another, it is sufficient if the influence of the original divine address is continued to us so that we ourselves learn of God what our present being and condition permit it to teach.

The Word as Truth appears to continue this divine influence successfully to this end. It presents to us what God is towards mankind, portrayed by the several ways in which He has made contact with humanity, culminating in the events of the life of Christ, and allows this to do what it may with our minds. There is no witness who declares that revelation forbids the free human understanding to operate, or that revelation ceases to be itself by permitting its operation. Wherefore, we cannot say that any fixable quantity or quality of content is divinely intended in any Word. It is to the whole of variable humanity that God speaks, and contact with His Word must issue in indefinitely variable results. Even the same person, considering that he is a living personality and not a static agent, and considering also the creative power of God's Word to increase the amenability of the hearer at any hearing, may never read the same passage twice with the identical result. But the variability of the results of God's address does not disprove the genuine character of the hearing. The knowledge of God which our present position and condition permit us to receive from Him will best serve to lead us nearer to

Himself. Rather should we say that whatever understanding of God is attained through sincere submission of our minds to this Word is precisely the content which God intends we should there and then receive. We cannot speak of the understanding of God in an absolute way, as either ours or not ours, but only of the deeper or shallower understanding of Him. The reception of the Word which reveals Him can only mean that our appreciation of Him is deepened by its influence. Wherever we may stand in point of the knowledge of God, if a difference in the right direction is made by His Word, it has prospered in the thing whereto it was sent, and we must then say that it has truly reached us.

4

When God reveals what He is through His demand upon men there is seemingly no division possible between the appreciation of the outward situations in continuity with which He is understood, and the appreciation of the content itself, which is God as known in continuity with them. For the category of demand unites God with what He demands, and His requirements have no meaning at all unless they are His. The possibility of stopping short at the familiarities presented to us, without in some degree understanding the divine nature of the content, does not seem to arise.

We may, therefore, advance at once to the question whether the knowledge which we thus acquire of God's Will can be adequate. Can we really know what God requires of us? Here, as elsewhere, the freedom of man's mind which revelation does not negate puts difficulties in the way. Yet here, as elsewhere, we cannot regard the consequences of divinely permitted freedom as fatal. The revealed Will of God serves the final divine end by leading us towards it and preparing us for it, and the process which prepares us for the regime of freedom which we must believe this divine end to be must leave us free to err while it leads us thither; and it is obvious enough that the individual precepts in which the revealed Will is expressed may sometimes induce a false understanding which works directly counter to the purpose of God. As one which may do so, the sixth commandment: "Thou shalt not kill", comes readily to mind. Since there are times when to refuse to kill would directly hinder the progress of Christian civilization, this prohibition cannot be rightly understood as an absolute for all times and conditions. But in a true sense the danger of atomism is only the danger of the unspiritual interpretation of the Word. The atomistic view may be spiritual in so far as it accepts this as a Word from God. But to take any precept as an absolute in itself is to regard it as a deposited truth which is an isolated occurrence complete in itself; pretty much as a biblical event may be falsely and unspiritually seen as a self-circumscribed occurrence, and to fail to take account of the whole event of God's approach of which it is only the termination or issue.

To be seen for what it really is, the precept must be seen as the issue of a particular divine approach. So seen, it reveals itself as a real expression of the requirements of the moral order which serves the divine end, but as an expression necessarily bound by the limits of abstraction; being such an abstract of this order as would secure for the divine purpose the best service possible from a community which could not, in its own religious condition, respond to a fuller revelation. It is one and the same circumstance, namely, the actual and particular contact of man with the divine moral order at a particular time, which at once renders any rationalized precept the real Word of God to us and also renders it a never final expression of the divine Will.

The atomistic interpretation is therefore false, not because of the rational form of the Word as truth, but because it fails to be the spiritual or prophetic view of the Word which we have found to be essential at all times. There is no danger in atomism when precepts reveal the requirements of the divine moral order to an extent greater than that to which we can respond; for example, with most of the precepts left by Christ. Consequently, these require, that they may profitably introduce us to God's Will, only that degree of spirituality which recognizes them as God's Word. But where the whole Christian revelation has given us an insight into the Will of God which transcends that derivable from any given particular precept, the spirituality required must go beyond atomism and view the single rationalization under the aspect of its true and historic place and significance. Only so will the written Word lead us to a profitable appreciation of what God requires of us in our present age.

Given the requisite spirituality, it would seem that the written Word does give us knowledge of God's Will. The Will of God, whether revealed in terms of an end or in terms of action, must be understood practically, in terms of human conduct, since it is what God requires of men to do. Of our own conduct, we have as immediate an awareness as it is possible to have of anything.

The warp and the woof, therefore, the material of thought out of which we may construct for ourselves an understanding of this Will under the synthetic guidance of the Word, is immediately to hand. Not that the perfect manhood and behaviour of Christ, Who finally reveals this Will, is so immediately known. The manhood and Love of Jesus are His own; not the manhood and love of the world to which He came. As the concrete realization before human eyes of that perfect human service to His purpose which might be said to exist archetypically in the mind of God, the manhood of Christ must transcend our understanding. But what Jesus Christ is within Himself would be more properly described as the perfect Desire of God than as the commanded Will of God which we must know. It is God's Will only in the sense of being His perfect Desire. It is not what God looks for from the men and women of the world; not what He expects or requires of them; and not, therefore, His actually commanded Will. If God's perfect Desire represented what we in our sin ought to do here and now by God's command, we should have to agree with Brunner that, for faith, "I ought" means "I am separated from the source of my origin and therefore cannot."[1] But the commanded Will of God is not what He would require of the perfectly regenerate in Christ, but what He does require here and now of the unregenerate; and the Kantian dictum: "I ought, therefore I can", must surely stand for faith as it does for Idealism.

What God calls us to do must surely be possible both to do and to understand. As embodying within Himself the perfect Desire of God, which is beyond both comprehension and emulation, Jesus Christ is still the Revealer of the commanded Will which we can both understand and obey. What was actually revealed by Christ to men and understood by them as His command was neither the perfect purity of His own Love nor yet merely the love of those to whom He commended it, but what came out of the tension between Himself and those whom He confronted. As men stood before the Love which could not be their own, their character and minds must have been influenced by it to understand a new human love which could be their own, and to appreciate this as God's demand of themselves. For they were convinced by Christ Himself that He commanded a new human love which He revealed and which they themselves must exercise. It seems, therefore, true to say that as *manifest* in the life of Christ the Will of God is revealed in terms of human conduct understood by those who knew Him in the flesh.

We should, then, be able to understand the Will thus made known at least as well as any other revelation. In so far as it differentiates between various types of conduct already familiar, it ought to be the most readily understood of all revelation. Negative precepts exclude what is known to the natural man and practised by him. Otherwise there would be no point in them. On the positive side, the revealed Will can at least begin its work of educating us to understand itself by dealing with the character

[1] *The Philosophy of Religion*, p. 91.

already in us. The precept "thou shalt love thy neighbour as thyself" encourages one familiar human tendency in contrast to its opposite, which is the method by which moral training naturally proceeds. By being held to the best standards that we can appreciate of inward feeling and outward action we are induced to develop morally, and to attain both a character and a practice inconceivable by us at the start. It is at least possible for the written Word, to begin with, to bring us to respect, if not always to practise, certain alternatives of feeling and action; and this in itself represents a definite gain and accomplishment of the Word. It is of the moral nature of man that he can possess an awareness of what he ought to be and do considerably in advance of what he actually is and does; while at the same time, whatever other forces may operate, this awareness does contain a power to induce action and develop character in keeping with itself. If the written Word can find a beginning, there seems no reason why it cannot lead us progressively to assimilate more and more of the pattern life of Christ.

It is, however, undeniable that since the Christian life is always an approximation to the divine-human life of Christ, though the degrees of approximation may be unlimited, it must always contain a quality of life and conduct which is new to the natural man, especially on its inward side. It can be strongly argued that unless the new manhood of the Christian fellowship begun by direct contact with Christ is preserved in a spiritual succession it must be lost, and that the written Word can do no more than define it to such as already know it in this succession. If there were no spiritual succession the Word might well be incapable of engendering any approximation to the life of Jesus. But we can scarcely put this to the test. It is hardly possible to deliver the Word to a humanity completely untouched by this life, which has made itself felt in unnumbered hidden ways through the institutions of the community.

The original Christian fellowship affects our ordinary life and practice in some degree, even if unsuspected and without being named for what it is, and we are all to this extent within it. But, while the written Word and the living Christian fellowship, self-declared or not, must work in unison, we are not dependent on the latter carrying the whole burden; nor can the limits of what is preserved as actual living example mark the limits of what the written Word can convey. If it were impossible at any time to conceive a better obedience to Christ than we can actually see, and possible only for the performance of Christian duty to deteriorate from this, the revelation in Christ would be a disheartening gift. The importance of living Christianity in preserving the meaning of the written Word cannot be minimized; but its supreme function would appear to be, not to present us with a maximum of faith or ethics which the Word can do more than define, but to give to the individual soul the necessary encouragement to live in the full freedom of its own God-given nature and not by its natural evil. Living in this freedom, we take our conception of Christian character, not from the human Christianity around us, but directly from the Christ portrayed in the Gospels. Having done its work of presenting the portrayed Christ to us in the form of our own conception, the mediacy of words drops out, and nothing at all appears to intervene between us and Jesus of Nazareth.

The question is, then, one which concerns our own God-given human nature in direct relation to the worldly Jesus. Are we or are we not capable of appreciating in any degree, for any degree is sufficient to start with, what He was or how He lived? Can our perception of Him—for more than conception seems possible—or, if not this, can our conception of Him, which is all that we need, be in any wise a true one? There are more assumptions about God, revelation, and man, in the denial than in the affirmation that humanity still has the capacity to conceive the worldly Jesus in some measure aright. Jesus Christ, as the revelation of God's Will, lived as He did, not only as revelation to the disciples, but as revelation to humanity of all time. The evangelists themselves knew Him through the Word passed on in the Christian fellowship, and wrote down what they learnt, without as much as questioning whether the mediacy of this act of theirs might be incapable of bringing others to learn rightly of the Christ they described. The assumptions behind the denial that we can thus learn of Him are contrary to the witness. The affirmation that we can and do involves only such assumptions as revelation itself must awaken us to perceive are not really such; but the serious recognition of what God achieves towards the human nature which takes its origin from Him, by the way He chooses, which is the way of the recorded life of the Word made flesh.

5

When we speak of its subjective aspect we embrace the essential character of revelation which Barth is so concerned to safeguard, namely, that God must personally address us in what we hear and learn of Him. The Content properly understood on its objective side must be *ipso facto* subjective, and if it cannot be so we agree that revelation does not get through. " 'God's Word' means 'God speaks'."[1] In his analysis of what this statement implies, Barth subsumes its implications under three main points: the spirituality, the personal character, and the purposiveness of the Word. It will be sufficient if we define how we believe the knowledge of God attained through the written Word gives contact with Him in the ways pointed out as necessary under these heads.

In the passage on "spirituality",[2] two points are clearly insisted on. We must have contact with the physis, or the inherent nature of the reality of God in His Word. This must, also, be contact with the physis of the right thing, of God; and not merely of the naturalness or corporeality involved in the worldly form of the Word. It is, then, claimed that for any other word than God's, physis signifies its limit. It may give us idealistic concepts without the reality, or the reality without the idealistic truth about it, but never both in their proper relation. Only in God's Word do we find the proper arrangement of spiritual and natural. By God's Word which succeeds in this we must of course here understand His direct, present address. The written Word, it is said, cannot give this contact with the spiritual reality of God. It is clearly held that any realism to which we attain by it is only the realism possible to fallen man; the physis of the movement, pressure, and impact of the worldliness of God's acts to the exclusion of their spirituality.

Since the Word comes to us as history, we may consider here also Brunner's remarks on the limitation of what the historian can grasp. History is viewed by Brunner as a masquerade.[3] We know that there is living decision and personality behind the acts that we see, and we know, even as critical philosophers, that life, conceived in terms of act, does not consist of pieces but is a unity. But, on Brunner's view, we no longer know rightly what there is behind the mask, which can never be removed. The historian cannot see the historical element proper, the vital decision, but only the after-history or consequence that more or less approximates to decision: like seeing the tree that is struck by lightning, but never the stroke of lightning itself.[4] If this were true of the history of human personalities, how much more so with God? The historian could give us only the events which mask Him, but in no wise the Personality behind the events. We might then be led to believe there was a Personal Unity behind the several events, but could never know this Unity.

We are here brought back to the question whether God can be known only by Himself alone, as a Unity amidst events which

[1] *Church Dogmatics*, I, p. 150, E.T.
[2] *Op. cit.*, pp. 151–154.
[3] *The Philosophy of Religion*, p. 122.
[4] *Op. cit.*, p. 121.

only mask Him, or whether He can be known as the Unity in and through events which do reveal Him as such. This is one and the same with the question whether we can have contact with the spiritual reality of God through contact with the worldliness of the events in which His acts terminate. Whether the written Word can give us this contact with the spiritual reality of God would seem to be properly this same question also. For while we must acknowledge the instrumentality of words, we must allow for their instrumental function, and for the living mind they stimulate. When words suggest to us a certain physis which they describe, the mind moves directly to this physis, if it accepts it, and relates itself directly to the real as best it can. Hence, the limit of the power of words to lead us to physis is the limit proper to the mind itself. Led by the words of biblical historical testimony, we are set the task of meeting with the spiritual physis of the events which they describe, through our own rational ordering of thought, and the question is whether this is possible. We note that Brunner goes so far as to say that we can "get at reality" in some way by an ordering process of thought, but emphasizes that what we are able to set in order is never more than a *datum* whose existence and nature finally evades comprehension; wherefore, we can never understand the true nature of reality in this way, this twofold result being the quintessence of critical idealism.[1]

It is true that in "idealistic" thinking we do order *data*, the physis of which we can never fully grasp. But the Barthian thought on this head again takes the oft-repeated line of first separating two inseparables; then arguing that experience of the one cannot be experience of the other; and, finally, demanding a rationalizing principle which we cannot supply ourselves in order to connect them, such as the present address of God. A *datum* is never a mere *datum*. It is only in theory that we can treat it as an isolable element of experience presented in an already defined form. While we appreciate the real, through ordering *data*, our reactive contact with the real conditions the formation of these *data*. At any time, the *data* which we set in order come to us as at least continuous with the reality whose inner nature escapes us, but which is, therefore, so far also a *datum*.

In the appreciation of history, *datum* and spiritual physis are especially inseparable. Bare events are not the *data* of history. Only meaningful events are so, events which of their own accord express the spiritual in act. If we understand the events of scripture at all, the spiritual Personality behind them ought to be apparent. It is indeed on the very ground that their relevance to a purposive Providence *is* apparent that they have been selected

[1] *Op. cit.*, p. 63.

THE IMPLICATIONS OF MEDIACY

and chronicled as scriptural history. The spiritual character of their revelation forces itself upon us in two ways. We appreciate the nature of God in and through what is other than God, and so far objectively. Yet even as we seek to understand Him thus, He cannot be objectified.[1] The history of both testaments speaks of a purposive Providence which, precisely because of its spiritual nature, transcends our capacity to define. We are thus compelled to speak of God as transcendent Spirit, while we contemplate, as objectively as possible, what history reveals His nature to be. But, over and above this, the coming of the written Word to us is itself part of the history that confronts us. The original approach of God extending to us, through time, in the form of this Word, is the *present* event of His speaking to us now in this way; even though it is not a new act of God, and even though we objectify the original approach as belonging to the past.[2] This present address affords us a direct appreciation of God as Spiritual, as we realize that it is He Who thus speaks to us, making possible the understanding of His nature in which also His Spirituality is appreciated. Thus, in two ways, the spiritual character of the Word refuses to be denied. It can be undeniable only because the physis, the Personality which addresses us and defies depersonalization by the understanding, actually does make contact with us.

It may be considered that we are simply acknowledging the kind of contact which is essential, and then interpreting the accomplishment of the written Word as this acknowledgment requires; and all that has been said may sound more like testimony than reasoned proof that it gives so much. But we are free agents, not static agents; and what matters is, that, as free agents, we should be able to rise to contact with the Personal God through what the written Word does with our minds. To show that this is possible is as much as can be done by any reasoning about a living awareness, and there appears nothing in the way of this possibility. We do not need to stop at an idealism out of touch with reality, since the rational processes of thought involved in the apprehension of God in His acts do not come between us and God. The concepts they yield are not something substituted for, but the instruments of, our noetic contact with Him.

Nor need we stop short at a realism which embraces only the worldly aspect of revelation. The *Imago* being still extant, if "a good thing spoiled", we can appreciate the nature of the Personal God as expressed by His acts, in receiving His Word as His. This

---

[1] See *Christ and the World of Thought*, by Prof. D. Lamont, Ch. VIII.
[2] This would be our *addendum* to the contention of Dr. Temple that personality is not immanent in past conduct, or in the record of it, and cannot be met with in these, but only inferred from them. See *Nature, Man, and God*, p. 285 ff.

must, of course, appear impossible to the Barthian view; for, if no worldliness can be made to express God or His message, we can know Him only through the category of causality, as an "unknown sort-of-a-something" that lies behind certain worldly events; and this is not to know God spiritually. But, from our standpoint, the worldliness of revelation does not stand between us and God, but is the overcoming of the gulf betwixt us and Him. It is essential, in order to express God's significance for human life, as Providence and Will.

If the written record of a divinely inspired history can bring the living spirit of man into contact with God as living and spiritual, as real and not merely ideal, every essential character of the Word, including its "personal character" and its "purposiveness", is secured.

We may, therefore, indicate only briefly how we stand with regard to the two specially named features which remain. Under the head of "spirituality" we were mainly concerned with the difficulties raised by the ontological mediacy, the worldliness, of revelation. Under that of the "personal character" of the Word it is the verbal form which Barth finds to be opaque. He allows the verbal form to stand instrumentally. "The personality of the Word of God signifies, not any diminution of its verbal character, but the sheerly active obstacle to reducing its verbal form to a human system, *i.e.*, to using its verbal form to lay the foundation and raise the structure of a human system."[1]

Since, for Barth, no human thinking at the bidding of the verbal form can ever do other than raise the structure of a human system, it must be deemed impossible in this way to make contact with God as God. Indeed, as a mere sign which may or may not be used by God, the verbal form has no intrinsic connection with God at all to proffer. Consequently, on Barth's view, if we make any use of it ourselves, we have at the outset abstracted from what we seek to find, and, beginning from what has no connection with God, can never find Him. Only the present address of God can give the Word the personal character it requires. "What God utters is never in any way known and true in abstraction from God Himself. It is known and true for no other reason than that He Himself says it, that He in Person is in and accompanies what is said by Him."[2]

But, on our part, we do not need to abstract from God while we take the verbal form of His Word as the basis and structure of human thought about Him. It has a twofold connection with God. As it guides us to conceive and thereby to appreciate spiritually what God is towards us, the verbal form possesses a connection

[1] *Church Dogmatics*, I, p. 157, E.T. [2] *Op. cit.*, p. 155.

with Him which no mere sign could ever have. It not only points, but leads, the mind to the reality which is God. And as we have noted, the Word as we have it is a speaking in which God is present, even though there is no renewal of the outward divine act from which it springs. We cannot see why the original presence of God in His Word must be lost simply by reason of the extension of His address through time. Whether the personal character or any other character of the Word gets home to us would seem to depend rather on the presence or absence of the fitting attitude in man. Neither the attitude described as the "I—my world" attitude, with which we perceive the purely objective aspect of things, nor the "I—thou" attitude with which we confront other persons, is sufficient. The "I—God" attitude is alone adequate to the appreciation of the fulness of revelation in any form.[1] But to this attitude, which is that of human faith, we would claim that the mediated Word does present itself as the direct address of God, the circumstance of its mediation being irrelevant either to its directness or to its personal character.

By the "purposiveness" of the Word of God, Barth means its pointedness. The sole way we know it is as the Word directed to ourselves as individuals, with something quite special to say to each one of us, and herein he names four essential points. God's Word is the Word we do not and cannot speak to ourselves, bringing a real encounter with God. It is the Word which aims at and touches us in our existence. It is the Word of reconciliation, which criticizes and establishes anew the relationship which exists between God and ourselves. Finally, as the Word which reconciles, it is the Word by which God "promises Himself as the content of man's future, as He who meets him on his way through time as the End of all time."[2]

What concerns us here is that it is argued that, because of its personal character, the Word can never be a truth;[3] and that because of its purposiveness towards the individual, the real content of God's speech, or the real will of the speaking person of God, must never be conceived or reproduced by us as a general truth.[4] What God is, does, and intends is certainly not a truth, but God's being and act. And it is, of course, essential to guard against any substitution of a mere truth for the pointedness of God's particular address to ourselves. But we cannot see why any such substitution need be involved in our conceiving the Word as truth, while it is also more than this; for to conceive it

---

[1] Cf. *Christ and the World of Thought*, p. 89 ff.
[2] *Church Dogmatics*, I, p. 161, E.T.
[3] *Op. cit.*, p. 155.
[4] *Op. cit.*, p. 159.

thus need not conflict with any of the essentials implied in its purposiveness.

Conceived as truth the Word is the Word whose agency is God and not ourselves, in which God aims at and encounters us where we now stand, in our present worldly thought and existence. It is the reconciling and redemptive Word not only by its quality as God's address, but also and especially by its form as truth. For, as it brings home to us the fact that we and the world are related to God, as God has made us to be; that we exist within the realm of His forgiveness and under His Providence, which intends a new existence to which it leads us, it opens to us this new existence. To teach us that this awaits us is to prepare us for it and lead us towards it. The creation of the new order involves the creation of a humanity which understands it, and it is the way of God proclaimed by Christ that whosoever receives the Word is as a friend and not as a servant, knowing what his Lord doeth; which signifies that, even now, the Word of God gives us to understand in a measure both the new order and the way in which God creates it; which is by recreating humanity through the Word.

This understanding which the Word is declared to give cannot conflict with anything else which it also gives. Why, then, should the Word which we now possess as truth be irreconcilable with any essential of the real Word? If it introduces us to a universal Providence it is only doing what the real Word must do; and, while we understand through it the nature of the new order and of its creation through the regeneration of man, this does not mean that we ignore the special and particular significance of God and His order for our individual selves; which is what we must mean by the pointedness of God's address to us as individuals. When we speak of the Will of God as a "general truth" we do not ignore this pointedness, but realize and acknowledge the universality of the moral order which inescapably embraces the whole of creation as it serves the abiding purpose of God.

We would thus urge that, in the spiritual reception of the Word of Truth, we may experience all that Barth emphasizes as essential to God's Word, including its spirituality, personal character, and purposiveness. We would urge further that the Word of God not only may, but must, be received as truth; indeed, as general truth. Stressing the necessity of living contact with God, Barth lays the emphasis entirely on its character as an address. But no address can be purely subjective. What is revealed can have no meaning unless we understand it to be the reality it is; and, for this, conceptualization is necessary. In revelation, we must come face to face with God, so far as we can. To the extent to which we can attain to "acquaintance" with God, conceptual articulation of what we apprehend Him to be may be unconscious, but must nevertheless be present. If it has to be consciously achieved, this may signify that the truth has not yet completed its work upon us, and that we do not yet know Him. But where there is no definition of His nature there is no knowledge of God at all. Further than the extent to which acquaintance is possible, we know only what we can clearly express in the form of truth.

In whatever way God reveals Himself, He is not adequately understood unless His universality is recognized, and this can be done only through concepts consciously defined and elaborated. The gracious attitude of God revealed to Isaiah is revealed as the universal attitude of God towards all humanity. Only, therefore, does the prophet proclaim it. The mere individuality of the address to him would have no significance for us. It is only because the attitude of God particularized towards him is universally a fact about our own existence that we can discern in it the pointedness of God's address to ourselves which comes through it. Only through its universality can we understand it at all. Not only so, but according to the revelation in Christ, God will not allow us to know Him in any other way. As is made clear by the opening words of the Lord's prayer, "Our Father", He will not allow us to know His Fatherhood nor to enter His Fellowship unless we appreciate how others also are sought by His attitude towards ourselves.[1] We cannot know God save as He who is disposed to all as He is to us.

The acknowledgment of the universality of God's goodness is thus integral to the acknowledgment of His address. To some extent we may be able to "feel" this divine love which is universal because it is pure. But we must acknowledge the divine goodness to be real far beyond our capacity to feel its reality, otherwise it is not the Fatherhood of God that we acknowledge. The necessity is laid upon us of confessing this Fatherhood which we cannot comprehend. We can appreciate it only by definitely saying to ourselves that it is universal; that it applies to all and not merely to some; that it is not passing but eternal. That is, the only possible way of acknowledging it is to define it and confess it as the truth.

Similarly with God revealed as Will. In a true sense the Will of God may be said to be unlimited, in as much as it is whatever God requires of this or that person at this or that time. But though unlimited and variable in its particular requirements, God's Will must be at all times what His purpose and divine moral order lays upon us. It must then be acknowledged in this universal aspect, as the significance for us now of this abiding Purpose and

---

[1] See Prof. J. Baillie, *Our Knowledge of God*, p. 178 ff.

order, or else it is not the purposive Will of God that is acknowledged; and again this universality can only be confessed as a truth. None can claim to perceive, to the extent to which he must confess its reality, either the good purpose or the moral Governance of God. Faith means the acceptance of this as beyond understanding, yet the definite acceptance of it as real. Hence in any revelation of the transcendent God, whether as Providence or as Will, the character of "truth" cannot be omitted, since only by confessing the truth about Him can we acknowledge Him adequately. The character of "truth" is as integral to the reception of the "address" as is the character of the address to the understanding of the truth. It is only in recognizing the pointedness of the address to ourselves that we can properly realize the serious significance for all of the divine self-relation to all. But at the same time it is the universal reality of God in His relation to the world which addresses us, and we must so recognize God in His address. We must receive the Word in both its characters, and we can receive it properly in either only if also in the other.

6

The function of "truth", to which Barth does not appear to do justice, is the function asserted by Aquinas in his tenet that in the last analysis revelation must commend itself to the human reason. Revelation makes its appeal to the whole man, reason included. No awareness of any kind seems possible without judgment, and what is revealed must commend itself to our judgment, winning our assent that it is real. The "Yes" or "No" with which we respond to God's approach is intellectual as well as moral. It may be that the intellectual "Yes" or "No" is ultimately dependent on our moral bearing, in as much as what we can appreciate must depend on what we ourselves are, morally and spiritually. But the intellectual pronouncement must be made, and made by ourselves. This being a human pronouncement, Barth cannot give it its due place and significance, and consequently cannot allow its proper value to the Word as truth. Since the intellectual pronouncement must be made by us, there is provided a distinct channel through which grace influences us, ministering to this necessity as the Word of truth. In whatever manner the assent to truth and immediate acquaintance with God may interact in regeneration, both must be present. We have acquaintance with God to a degree, and the character of truth becomes subordinate in so far as we do succeed in becoming acquainted with Him. But this circumstance seems to illustrate an economy of effort, rather than to show that the character of "truth" can be dispensed with even here. Assent is real even though it be completely won and without need of renewal as we stand in the presence of God.

We must agree that without direct acquaintance "truth" could not be the statement of reality in the form of propositions. The Thomist position must be supplemented by the Barthian emphasis on the real presence of God. But the Barthian position must be modified by the Thomist emphasis on truth, in so far as no acquaintance with God is possible save through the rational apprehension of His nature. We must confess God's Fatherhood, His Will, His transcendence in every aspect, as a truth in which we believe. This does not mean, however, that the apprehension of God is possible only in belief. It has been urged that a view which claims "knowledge" of God and not merely "belief" in Him is too optimistic, and that only "belief" is possible.[1] But a belief which is only that, and no more, can stand on no firm ground; and were we to yield to this criticism we would be surrendering the whole value of the mediacy of God's Self-disclosure. To have real belief in God we must definitely know Him at some point, and this the mediacy of revelation permits. God approaches us in those ways in which we can know Him, wherefore the truth of His transcendence, as the truth concerning Him Whom we know, is of real and not merely ideal significance.

It would be altogether impossible to attempt to define where knowledge ends and where the belief which is real because of it begins, but each is essential that the other may be effective. By His own grace we meet with the God Whom we cannot comprehend, yet do meet with Him in this way: the necessity of confessing the transcendence which we cannot grasp being the sign that we *have* met with God, not the sign that we have not done so. As we confess the transcendent reality of God, we neither confess Him as a proposition, not yet grasp His transcendence, but withal are directly aware of Him. There is no contradiction in the claim that we are directly acquainted with Him Who transcends understanding.

[1] See review of "Our Knowledge of God" in *Theology*, January, 1940, p. 70.

IX

THE WILL OF GOD AND THE CHRISTIAN METAPHYSIC

I

God's Word is at once a personal address and a Word of Truth. Theology may emphasize either of these aspects, the change of emphasis from the one to the other partly explaining the difference between the older and what is commonly termed the "new" theology. The character of the Word as a personal address undoubtedly used to command more attention than it now does. The aspect of truth could never be ignored, but because of the emphasis on the personal element the truth which interested former theology was that which comes to light when we look inwardly and directly towards God. How the individual stands towards God, in this life and the hereafter, is the main interest. Sin considered as disobedience, vital decision, forgiveness, election, regeneration and personal salvation are dominating categories. The Will of God, contemplated mainly as within the bounds of the personal relationship, tends at times to be defined without reference to any disclosure of itself in the outside world. The inclusion of the outside world in the divine scheme of things, as affected by and relevant for the purpose of Providence, appears to have been accepted, as it must be to justify any missionary enterprise which aims at the well-being of the world, without overmuch thought or discussion. Following a general change in outlook, thought has tended to become more metaphysical. The meaning of Providence; what it means for the world that God is God; how God influences the world; man's destiny, and his progress towards it, have become central questions. They cannot be otherwise for those who seriously feel the necessity of reconciling worldly events with the belief in Providence. Such questions concern what we have held to be the subject-matter of revelation, how God has related Himself to the world of men. The significance of His relation to man is what we mean by the spiritual cosmos in which our lives are set. Thus, a right understanding of revelation discloses to us what ought to be the Christian Metaphysic. As we see it, the function of the Word includes that of guiding us to live and to do as God's purpose requires through giving us a *knowledge* of the conditions of our life and being, which are determined by His Good Purpose. The revealed Will is the definition of these conditions in terms of their direct significance for human conduct.

THE WILL OF GOD AND THE CHRISTIAN METAPHYSIC

It declares what our total environment demands of us for the realization of our destiny in God.

If we are to maintain this, these conditions must be permanent. If God should affect the world only from time to time there would be no practical value in our taking account of His relation to us. We can proceed to do so only upon the conviction that the Transcendent God is always relevant for the world, and that the world is always relevant for God, or, alternatively, that there is no escape from the divine Governance, what we do or leave undone being always relevant one way or another for the fulfilment of the divine end. This means that by God's decision the realm of nature is unified with the realm of Grace. This is denied by Barth, and we must justify our assertion of the divine unification of these realms.

2

The problem of how the realm of nature is related to the realm of grace is fundamentally the problem of divine immanence, since it concerns how God "touches" the world. In the *Credo* (p. 34), Barth defines the immanence of God as "His free, omnipotent presence and lordship in the world that He created"; this presence and lordship being such that "God never and nowhere becomes the world. The world never and nowhere becomes God." Within the limit of the Word in the flesh, and only within this limit, God "stands over against the world". "In standing over against the world that He has made, God is present to it; not only far but near; not only free in relation to it but bound to it; not only transcendent but also immanent." The first concern of this statement is, obviously enough, to safeguard the free lordship and independence of the transcendent God. But one is left wondering whether the fear of pantheism or immanentism has not prevented any effective meaning being allowed to immanence. Is immanence to be exhaustively explained as the mere presence of a transcendence which remains pure transcendence even while it is near? Does God's standing over against the world as other than the world constitute the whole meaning of His immanence? Or, on the other hand, is the way in which God stands over against the world to be itself explained by a real immanence; by an entry of God into the human cosmos which unifies it permanently with the transcendent divine order? The point is as to *how* God binds Himself to the world.

Barth has made his position clearer in the *Dogmatics*.[1] The "touching" of the world by God holding only within the Word,

[1] See *Church Dogmatics*, I, pp. 173–184, E.T.

all that is said of the relation of the Word of God to the individual must be said also of the relation of God to the human cosmos in general. The Word itself is not permanent but a spasmodic occurrence. Consequently, the significance of God for the world is only operative from time to time. Only from time to time are the human cosmos and the acts of man related by God's decision to the transcendent divine order and made relevant for the divine end to be realized through it. Consequently, we must not even say that the world is the victim of its own godlessness. Human acts in themselves are irrelevant, either as obedience or as sin, to the realization of God's transcendent purpose. Only by His specially directed grace does the opportunity come to us of being believers or unbelievers, of being obedient or disobedient to His Word. Previously and *per se* we have not the slightest chance of being either the one or the other. But, God's decision about the world once made, the heathen are "on the way to Mount Zion", whether they know it and desire it or not. Hence the only permanency about God's binding of Himself to the world is the abidingness of His *transcendent* purpose. The power of the divine $\tau\acute{\epsilon}\lambda o\varsigma$ to break through the existing discontinuity and to relate to itself the otherwise unrelated world is all that immanence, God's touching of the world, can be said to mean. Further, it is obviously essential to this view that the divine purpose is unconcerned with this world. For human actions have their effect on the world's future by their own causality, without the necessity of a new divine decision that they shall do so; and cannot fail to be relevant for God's purpose unless its scope lies entirely outside the worldly sphere.

The position is even more stringently stated by Dr. Camfield, by whom immanence is defined as the presence of transcendence, with enquiry not as to the how, but only as to the limits of this presence. Much is made of the tenet that not only man but also nature is involved in the fall.[1] It is asked what need there can be for a new creation, if the laws of nature are already the workings of the creative spirit. The discontinuity between God and His own created nature is maintained with such thoroughness as to include the statement that there are definite limits to the range and power of miracle, and the even more surprising statement that death is an evil.[2] It is denied that Christ "broke through the world reality limited through death, by miracle in His resurrection", and asserted that He accepted this limitation. Only "in the bearing of it" did He take it away.[3] All of which we take to mean that only within the event of Christ's coming is discontinuity super-

---

[1] *Revelation and the Holy Spirit*, p. 148 ff.
[2] *Op. cit.*, p. 136.
[3] *Op. cit.*, p. 137.

THE WILL OF GOD AND THE CHRISTIAN METAPHYSIC

seded by relatedness. His advent, death, and resurrection apparently achieve no permanent relatedness of God to the world. As past events which we can understand, they only point us to the difference between God and ourselves, and to a gulf between the natural and the divine order which God may overcome from time to time.

The processes of thought by which this Barthian position is supported seem far from convincing. As we observed in reference to Aquinas, the independence of God is not jeopardized when He binds Himself to the world by His own choice; His free lordship would not be endangered, as seems to be supposed, by a more thoroughgoing immanence than Barth allows. If God remains free while He binds Himself to the world at all, He remains free however He binds Himself, and His lordship is the more, not the less, significant if it means a permanent unification of the natural with the divine order. Again, while it is obviously true that only by God's grace are we given the opportunity of obeying and serving, this in itself cannot determine the limits within which this opportunity actually is given. The opportunity to serve is not spasmodic just because God must give it. Similarly, while it is true that it is by the coming of God in Christ that the division between God and the world is broken down, and by the Resurrection that the evil of death is taken away, it does not follow that the achievement of these divine acts is confined to the times of their occurrence. The bridging of the gulf is accomplished by miracle, that is, by God's act; but no limitation of the range and power of miracle is justifiable on the strength of this observation.

Such, however, are only supporting considerations which presuppose the position for which they argue. The real reason why this theology of crisis has to postulate a renewed act of God to render our endeavours relevant to His purpose is that it begins by doing less than justice to what God's relation achieves. In whatever way the supposed discontinuity is expounded, the previously quoted remark of Gogarten appears equally cogent at every turn. The human cosmos is considered in isolation from God at the start, and the isolated character which it would have without God's relation to it is contemplated as still surviving despite this relation, and as continuing thereby to present the same limits to God's grace as would have obtained without it. "Reality is not ignored, not set aside, not disqualified, not dismissed, but is accepted in its own quality",[1] by God. Because the power of sin is contemplated as unaltered by God's approach to man, sin must in the end be dismissed and set aside when God speaks. Because the human cosmos remains entirely opposed to God, no service

[1] *The Word of God*, p. 89.

to the divine end can be rendered through the context which it provides.

The acceptance of the world by God, His taking it under His care and relating it to His purpose, is what we mean by Providence. For Barth, Providence means here and now no more than the promise and possibility of the divine τέλος relating the world and our actions to itself. But the very terms of God's self-union with the world seem to point to a much fuller meaning of Providence, as God's acceptance of the world by a permanent adoption. The terms are those of Love and Will, and we must take account of what these imply. Since, according to the evangelists the work of Christ inaugurated a New Age (αἰών), we must ask what they mean as perfected through Him. First of all, can this new adoption through Christ mean no more than a new promise and a new possibility of undoing the work of sin and relating us to God's purpose? Or is it the realization of a new relationship? If the latter, we may then ask whether God's purpose relates to this present world, and in what way the Word as truth guides us towards the realization of the divine end in this sphere.

The Love of God declared in Christ culminates in the Forgiveness of sin as the central and paramount theme of the New Testament. Forgiveness is God's reply to sin and its effects, and it is in it as perfected and symbolized in the Cross that we must find the ultimate answer to the contention that sin has caused a separation of the natural order from the order of redemption. In a sense, Barth is undoubtedly right in saying that Christ accepted sin as sin, and likewise death as death. But while He accepted both in their own quality, He at the same time accepted them as evils to which He was the divine answer, and the answer which altered their significance. Sin continues to mean, despite Christ's acceptance of it, that God's Will actually is not done where His reconciliation is spurned and His Word unheeded. Thus forgiveness, which like all revelation does not complete its work except as it wins our response, does imply a promise and a possibility. But the promise and possibility which it implies refer not to itself, but to ourselves and the fruits of our response to it. Forgiveness cannot be the promise of itself. It must be realized on God's side before it can bring any new dynamic to our moral and spiritual life, and before it can begin to hold out any further possibilities. Forgiveness as God's answer to sin being already real, we may then hold or not, as we choose, that the effects of sin are cosmic, involving not only fallen man but a fallen nature, though we find it difficult to give a real meaning to this latter conception. But if sin is held to be cosmic in its effects, we are entitled to say that God's forgiveness is also cosmic in its effects.

If the fall and forgiveness mean something for the ontology of the universe, we cannot examine directly what they thus mean. We can only say what they mean for ourselves and our response to revelation. If sin as a cosmic phenomenon means that the opportunity of serving God by obedience to His Will is lost to us, forgiveness cannot mean less than that it is restored. For forgiveness relates directly to the opportunity of service, and is unmeaning if it does not open the door to it. The reconciliation of the Cross would be a mockery if it did not bring us the opportunity of retribution for wrongs and of furthering the divine end by devotion to the Will of the God to Whom we are reconciled. Wherefore we must believe in the restoration, if lost, of the situation in which obedience to God's Will is possible by our own choice of gratitude.

It may be doubted whether the Barthian theology does full justice to the truth of Forgiveness. We underrate the divine achievement if we say that the Cross does no more than point out the discontinuity between the world and what lies on the other side of death and resurrection. Grace overcomes the limits which it accepts. The Cross signifies the actual bridging of the gulf in reference both to the present fellowship of man with God and to the relevance of human acts for His purpose. It is God's limitation of the way in which sin obstructs His Will, which it still does by preventing human service, though not by removing the possibility of service. It is God's decision between the alternatives we named: between a Providence which is only transcendently possible and a Providence already actual as a new relationship between Himself and the world. We do not now need to wait for God to act, in order that obedience to the Word we hear and know in Jesus Christ may become relevant to the divine end. The cosmically effective decision is already made, by God, in this same Word. The decision which remains to be made, to determine whether or not our actions are to be a genuine service, is our own. The New Age has placed us in a new world in which the call to serve never ceases to confront us as an abiding challenge. And the divine cosmic decision already made, which alone renders our own decision relevant, is of such a kind that it can determine what our own is to be. "One who looks up into the face of a forgiving God is set within a world of new realities, his personal response to which is the Christian morality . . . in Christ he beholds fully and persuasively revealed that will of God which he is called to know and obey."[1]

The revelation of God as the divine Love which forgives thus declares that God has bound the world to Himself, and that it

---

[1] H. R. Mackintosh, *The Christian Experience of Forgiveness*, p. 121.

remains so bound despite the fact of sin. The revelation of God as Will likewise declares what sort of a binding this is. From the very first the difference between Yahweh and pagan deities was recognized as the difference between a Providence which operates in concert with the responsive obedience of men and one which bestows its blessings otherwise. The early pagan worship of Palestine consisted almost entirely of offering sacrifices to deities, to whom all obligation appears to have ceased with the completion of the act of worship. But at Kadesh, the chief sanctuary, the altar of Yahweh was identified with the seat of judgment.[1] Yahweh had not finished with His people when they left His altar. His purpose was to be attained through their obedience in doing what He required of them. Sin and obedience are in a double sense opposition to and conformity with God's Will. We indicate only half the truth when we describe sin as the defiance of His personal address. Inwardly it is so, but sin is sin because outwardly it is also the obstruction of God's purpose, by what it does in the world. Obedience is inwardly a loyalty to an address, but is also outwardly a compliance as furthering this purpose by the effects of its deeds. And when we look at the kind of actions which God requires of us, we find they are not chosen at random.

Apart from injunctions of an obviously temporary import, there is nothing commanded in the Old Testament or enjoined by the precepts of Christ, unless its practice is both good in itself and leads to further and recognizable good beyond itself. Nor is there anything condemned as sin unless its practice at once offends our conscience as evil and leads to further evil. The nature of the actions which God requires of us seems to make it quite plain that He desires us to further what is at once our own good and His purpose through the effects of our actions in this world. His Will is meaningless unless the life it calls for actually does lead towards the end He desires. Is there not here manifested God Who works providentially at all times, being immanent in the laws of the spiritual world He has made, which are as truly the natural laws of our being as those that are sheerly natural? God revealing Himself as Will, Providence is manifest as the provision of a moral and spiritual medium within which we are set the task of working towards the attainment of his desires, and also as the divine Governance by which the life of endeavour thus defined by His Will inevitably leads towards this attainment, and the conduct condemned as sin just as inevitably in the opposite direction. The Will of God implies this providential immanence as the ground of its relevance. It implies the whole spiritual reality in which we

[1] See *The Preparation for Christ in the Old Testament*, Bible Class Series, Vol. I, Ch. V.

live, move, and have our being, defining the significance of this for the practical life of faith. It describes the life of vocational endeavour which the world we live in renders indispensable for our own good and the divine end, and what actions it renders the reverse. Providence is thus what determines the causal connections between obedience to God's Word and the attainment of His Good, which includes ours, and also what determines the causal connection between sin and evil. These causal connections cannot be operative from time to time only. They are part of creation, "written in the nature of things".

It seems clear enough, also, that the divine purpose we are called to serve embraces the world we know. The view that our present world is no more than a moral and spiritual training ground for participation in a higher existence has never gained universal acceptance. A more direct manner of preparation for eternal life is conceivable, and surely the creation of the world has a purpose and meaning of its own. Scripture does indeed imply (John iii. 16) that the supreme aim of God's love to the world is to win us for Himself eternally, but the love shown forth in Christ is directed immediately to men in their present existence, and values uprightness of heart and hand here and now for its own sake. At no time is our present world made to appear of no intrinsic value in God's sight; wherefore we prefer to believe that the love of God is directed to this world as included within the scheme of providence. God plainly wills that we seek the good of the world we live in, and we could not seriously obey this Will unless the world were properly an end for God as well as for ourselves. To ask whether He bids us do so because its welfare is itself part of His purpose in a final sense, or only as if it were so in order that we may thereby attain the character sought by His grace, would be to present a false alternative by splitting the divine intention which is one. We cannot succeed in presenting a character acceptable to God by directly aiming to offer it, whether for the sake of securing our personal salvation, or even for the sake of offering it to God. The filial attitude of faith which is finally acceptable to Him is surely to be attained only through compliance with His Will, which bids us look not only inwardly towards Himself but outwardly to the world whose welfare is the concern of His love.

The divine Love and Will declared in the scriptures thus imply that our relation to God is abiding. The contrasting Barthian view uses its broad conceptions of the effacement of the *Imago*, and of a natural order out of touch with the divine, as if they represented primarily knowable facts which must determine everything that is to be said about our practical religious situation. But we cannot deduce practical consequences from such conceptions. They are neither a proof nor, ultimately, even an explanation of what the practical facts of life are, but only idealistic summaries of what Barthianism believes them to be. Only when stated in terms of the practical possibilities open to us have they any clear meaning. Does the conception of an effaced Imago clearly mean anything except that we cannot hear God's Word? And does the separation of the natural from the divine order mean anything, except that voluntary service on our part is of no consequence for the divine purpose? Questions about the practical possibilities of the religious life can only be answered directly, by reference to what the Word of God says about them. The union of the two orders which revelation declares and achieves is above all a practical union. It is indeed scarcely intelligible otherwise. Through Christ, God relates the world of human endeavour to His ultimate purpose; so that there is now no possibility of placing ourselves outside the realm in which all human action in response to His Word is relevant, one way or the other, for the divine end. It would no doubt be excessive optimism to say that the natural order is *ipso facto* one with the order of redemption. But to affirm that the two are made one through grace is only to take revelation seriously with all its consequences.

3

The Christian revelation claims to set before us the only aim of life which is at once rational and complete. It claims further to provide the only dynamic of progress that will suffice, since it alone takes account of all the relevant factors of our total environment and urges us to face up to them. It expresses the nature and conditions of our being in terms of their significance for life and practice. It takes account of God, Who requires us to seek the good of the world; also of the transcendent divine end, the nature of which is only dimly conceivable by us, but which can be served by pursuing the good of the world we know; and which is, therefore, sufficiently defined for us in the way which is practically necessary, in terms of the endeavour by which we are required to serve it on earth. We know at least that we are required here and now to work for a civilization which harmonizes with our adoption by God, and that this can neither be created nor sustained save by the life defined in His Will.

Revelation also takes account of human sin as insufficiently recognizable, whether as to its extent or its nature, by any worldly ethic which pursues a merely human end as if it were the complete and final end of our being. Thus, while it proclaims that our world, spiritual and moral, is so constituted that obedience to the divine Will is inexorably the only road to our true human destiny, it offers us its practical guidance whereby the hindrances that arise from within our nature may be overcome, and our energies harnessed to serve God's purpose in spite of them. St. Luke has summarized the whole Will of God by expressing in one sentence the first and greatest commandment and the second like unto it, thereby emphasizing their inseparability. "Thou shalt love the Lord thy God with all thy heart, and with all thy soul, and with all thy strength, and with all they mind; and thy neighbour as thyself."[1] The very terms in which the first commandment is expressed—"with all thy heart, soul, strength and mind"—indicate that inward love to God necessarily embraces the outward life of thoughtful and purposive action defined in the second as equitable love to one's neighbour, for the accomplishment of which a filial attitude to God is essential. Purposive good-will, in which we may perfect ourselves by constant communion with God through Christ, from whose earthly life we learn it, is thus enjoined upon us as the universally essential means of our progress towards the end which God desires. The promise that this way of life is sufficient for the end it must serve is implicit in the Will which commands it.

It is frequently said that the revealed Will is too general, lacking the detail requisite for practical guidance in concrete situations. It obviously must abstract from particular situations. Otherwise it would have to lay before us the whole story of man from beginning to end, including the definition of every single problem as well as that of its solution. This is impossible, not only for other obvious reasons, but because history is indeterminate. Since the incongruity of evil in the spiritual order is free to present us with whatsoever perplexities it may devise, the problems that may confront us, and their precise solutions, are unpredictable contingencies. Revelation does not define the solutions of specific problems, but teaches us the attitude and bearing of Christ with which we must meet them. Yet, in so far as sin manifests itself in certain definable and recurrent human tendencies, the goodwill which overcomes them is portrayed as a moral endeavour correspondingly variable in character. The several ways in which we are enjoined to combat anti-social sin in ourselves all consist of the substitution of love, in one form or another, for selfishness or hate; the detailed precepts of the Will being particularizations in divers regards of the one basic principle stated in its summary.

This essential spirit of Christian endeavour is naturally discoverable only through its practice, in the course of which the

[1] Luke x. 27.

guidance of the revealed Will is bound to become more specific as we deliberately ask ourselves its meaning for particular situations. Until we do so it can be of no practical value. Far from negating the human personality, the Will of God depends on the operation of its faculties for its own achievement. "Thou shalt" is addressed to living persons, and the "thou" must live, not only as it obeys, but also as it hears the Word of God. It would be obviously irrational to take account of the particular circumstances of any concrete situation in assessing what we need and expect to receive from His Word, and then to omit these factors from the hearing of it which determines what we receive. Consulted as a Word addressed to us in the situation which actually confronts us, the Will of God should be specific enough; its essential spirit, which we discover in proportion as we strive to acquire it, connecting with the particular acts to be done, which we discover in proportion as we seek to do them.

The circumstance that our human faculties must operate both in the understanding and in the discharge of Christian duty means that error is not only possible but doubly probable. Only gradually can revelation give to the world the capacity to benefit from what it has to teach. Thus not only are the finer methods of creative Christian effort imperfectly conceived by us, but even what we understand of them is frequently impossible to apply. Neither prophet, Christ Himself, nor apostle, ever pretended that the world was in a more advanced stage than they found it to be; and according to their example the means of the world's redemption adapts itself to actual conditions. The appointment of Saul as king, a man of no brains whatever for social construction, whose only service was that of co-ordinating force; the clearing of the temple; the warning against casting pearls; and the indication of possible impracticability with which St. Paul qualifies his injunction to live peaceably with all men; are instances which show how both Testaments recognize that the spirit of good-will must turn to whatever methods of attaining its aim are left open by the sin which it combats.

All this increases the probability of error. We can tell in retrospect whether our efforts have brought forth good, but we cannot always recognize in prospect what will do so. Yet the value of revelation remains. The good-will which errs in its endeavours is still led by the Will which it imperfectly obeys. The promise contained in the Will is not that we shall not err. Rather is it that by curbing the harmful tendencies within us and using our natural powers under the influence of Christ we shall serve the divine end to the best of our capacity, which is all that God requires of us. His providential relation to us means that such endeavour of ours, errors or no errors, is sufficient for the progressive realization of His purpose. It is therefore sincerity, not accuracy of foresight, which is the first essential. The foresight required of us is such as we may possess. But the universal commandment is absolute in its demand for sincerity. Love is by its very nature sincere.

The sufficiency of the revelation which God extends to us is due to its being directed to overcoming sin itself, the source of evils; not merely to rectifying certain specific evils. The worst afflictions of this world do not arise because the Word of God leaves us in doubt as to what line of action will best serve Him. The untoward results which may at times follow honest effort can be regarded as of secondary significance only. The main and root cause of the sufferings of humanity may be broadly described as the absence of good-will and the persistence of egotism which is undebatably immoral, and for the religious mind the flagrant violation of the plain meaning of the Will of God. The sin that matters acts not in doubt whether it serves God's Will, but in the full knowledge that it opposes it. The conflict is between two forces, each of which recognizes where it stands and acts as it does because it stands where it does. There is the force of progress, which trusts that the Supreme Mind which sets us the task of life can alone declare to us how this task is to be fulfilled, and which believes that the way of life portrayed in the manhood of Christ is at one with the ultimate power behind the universe. The other, the force of sin itself, is that which would persuade us to follow any inclination as if questions of right and wrong were irrelevant, towards whatever kind of destiny is then conceivable. Fundamentally, it is the conflict between God and sin. In us, it is the conflict between the purposive good-will which the Living Word of God calls forth in us, and the amoral or immoral adventures of irresponsible experiment. By the Love of God extended to us through Christ, we live in the order of redemption. As the Love of God in Christ wins the hearts of men and abides in them, so is the purpose of this order realized.

4

We have sought to maintain that God, in His providential self-relation to us, discloses Himself in such a way that problems concerning the hearing of His Word and obedience to it are overcome from the divine side, so that in our present state we may both understand and do what God now requires of us. The call to serve is addressed to the sinner, and to the saint as aware of himself as a sinner. The sincere endeavour to respond is divinely guided, even though it errs.

The Barthian theology, which finds in our sin an insurmountable obstacle to the intrinsic value and relevance of spontaneous hearing and obedience, surely does less than justice to the grace with which the Word is given and less than justice to the Love in which service is asked. The more one reads of Barth, the more one becomes convinced that his thought does not really start from an appreciation of God's work in Christ, however much he insists that it is here we must begin. The real starting point appears to be the conviction that the *Imago Dei* is not merely defaced but effaced. This strongly suggests that disillusion is at least one cause of the preliminary despairing attitude which Barth shares with his predecessor Kierkegaard. Kierkegaard's thought represents the natural reaction of a disillusioned spiritual mind to the theology which preceded him. Schleiermacher, whose work Barth regards as a misfortune, had taught that God was to be found through analysis of our mental states. This is sound enough when understood to mean that we may thus discover how God has touched us. But this method of approaching the problem of the knowledge of God prepared the way for the method of speculative rationalism, which proceeded as if the human nature examined were itself God. Attempting to determine too much by examining too little, the rationalists could not but fail to appreciate the essential character of the divine. Hegel and Strauss practically identified the divine spirit with the human, dissolving the individuality of man in the process. Nor could they appreciate the essential character of the religious life as a spiritual response to God. God being regarded as impersonal, and the significance of human individuality being set aside, the sense of sin especially was bound to be obscured, depending as it does on the individual's awareness of responsibility to God as a Person.

Kierkegaard's theology was worked out in opposition to the Hegelian system. It is, as we should expect, that he gave an almost exaggerated prominence to the spiritual seriousness formerly obscured, and only natural that one so acutely alive to sin should have stressed the renunciatory aspect of the Christian life at the expense of the positive aspect. His melancholy temperament alone would suffice to explain his despair of man and his works. The influence of Karl Marx, who regarded despair as an indispensable dynamic of progress in the social and political world, may unconsciously have helped to confirm him in the conviction that despair is an essential religious dynamic. He held that self-despair is the only possible way of giving ourselves to God, and must continue throughout the life of faith. As self-despair is a form of self-negation, we are already on the way to the view that the suppression of the self is the first thing God asks of us.

THE WILL OF GOD AND THE CHRISTIAN METAPHYSIC

It is only a short step from extreme emphasis on the need for a passionate self-surrender to God to the position that God, acting purely and by Himself, is responsible not only for the initial decision to serve Him but for everything in the life of faith, to the exclusion of all human initiative. This further step was taken when Kierkegaard's thought was developed by Barth. It is not surprising that another intensely religious and spiritual temperament should have gone so far. Since Kierkegaard's time we have witnessed chaotic failures of human enterprise. Desolation has been wrought by creeds and movements purporting to be the means of establishing a new and better order, and Barth's disillusioning experience of the perversion of the human soul may have been as shattering as Luther's.

Emphasis on spirituality need not, of course, lead to such a view as Barth's, though it evidently does so for those predisposed in this direction by an attitude of despair born of disillusion. We can welcome the insistence on spirituality without accepting the distinctive Barthian tenets which separate the world from grace—in part, doubtless, because the social and political experiences which tend to produce this attitude have affected us less than others. We have, so far, been spared the worst of Europe's turmoils. This circumstance, backed by our different theological background, may go far to explain why the influence of Kierkegaard, and in a lesser degree the influence of Barth himself, has been slow to make itself felt in this country. Hegelian rationalism has never dominated our theological thinking. Indeed, the system of Hegel has scarcely been so much as mentioned in many of our church colleges. On the other hand, the evangelical preaching of a new moral life, attainable by the sinner through direct regenerative relationship with God, has never allowed the problem of the knowledge of God to fall out of its essentially spiritual context, as happened with the Hegelians.[1] Consequently, though Kierkegaard brought an understanding of the problem of the knowledge of God which was new to the majority of German thinkers, he cannot be said to have done so for those of evangelical tradition. To such, his message must have been so much the less arresting from the outset, whence it would naturally receive the less attention. Similarly, to-day, the average reader of Barth in this country cannot but feel that at times he is fighting battles that have been already won.

Besides Kierkegaard, Barth claims the ancestry of Luther, Calvin, St. Paul, and Jeremiah.[2] To these, others might be added; for the tendency to separate the world from grace, in one way or

[1] See H. R. Mackintosh, *Types of Modern Theology*, Ch. VII.
[2] *The Word of God*, p. 195.

another, is a recurrent phenomenon in the history of Christianity, and is still apparent in several sects of the present day. Human nature may be viewed as incapable of anything good, so that all that appears praiseworthy to most of us is regarded as evil; as, with the followers of Judge Rutherford, for whom "religion" is the great enemy of God. Or it may be thought capable of receiving certain divine gifts, and of performing by grace works good in themselves, though incapable thereby of extending to others the grace received. With the Irvingites, for example, grace is limited to the elect, who cannot be missionary in the creative sense of the word, their apostolic labours being confined to warning such as are already chosen of the coming Day of the Lord. Or not only man but created nature may be viewed as inherently evil, as with the Gnostic sects. But whether man, nature, or both are taken to be satanic, the result is that the present world tends to be regarded as unfit to be the object of divine interest, and religious life tends accordingly to be withdrawn from it.

A primary concern of the early Gnostics was to find a theory of the cosmos which would avoid attributing to God any responsibility for evil. They accordingly conceived the Demiurge as the author of the material universe and of man, both being inherently evil. Redemption consisted of deliverance from the world, and though man was said to help towards his deliverance by asceticism and faith, faith was not conceived as the reception of divine aid, but merely as the expectation of deliverance. Revelation, or γνῶσις, was purely a divine gift which bestowed a higher life. According to Clement of Alexandria, in proportion as man attained this higher life he ceased to be man and became "like a god". In the form of Manichæism, Gnosticism became infused with many ideas from eastern religions, and was embraced in this form by Christian sects well into the middle ages. The Albigenses ostensibly professed the Manichæan philosophy. They affirmed a dualistic origin of matter and spirit, evil matter being eternal. Here we have a parallel to the "fallen Cosmos" of Barth. Mankind is said to be the creation of the powers of darkness, which gives us a parallel to the effacement of the *Imago Dei*. All contact with matter being a defilement, it was taught that the Christ of the evangelists was an emanation of the spirit of evil, who sought to undo the work of the true Christ in heaven. In this we have a parallel to the Barthian view which confines the *locale* of revelation to the risen and exalted Lord. The ideas of a sinful cosmos and of revelation confined to the transcendent sphere are not Christian but pagan in origin.

It is in respect of the origin of evil that Manichæism most

THE WILL OF GOD AND THE CHRISTIAN METAPHYSIC

sharply contrasts with the teaching of Jesus, who has nothing to say about an evil origin of man, and nothing to say about a primordially evil cosmos, or even about a fallen one. These twin tenets shield man from responsibility as much as they shield God. Christ did not come to redeem us from an evil which has its source outside ourselves. He may have shared the popular belief in a personal devil, and would not have denied that temptation may come from without. But it is the sin that lies within, for which we cannot deny responsibility, from which He sets us free, redemption beginning with the confession of guilt. The pronouncement made by Archbishop Gerbert against the Albigenses, that he believed in an evil spirit *non per conditionem, sed per arbitrium* expressed the change which Christ brought to the world's conception of the evil which matters. This evil is not cosmic, but is the sin of man's free will.

When it is recognized that sin originates in the human will, it ought to be recognized also that withdrawal from the world is not essential for the good life. Neither Luther nor Calvin were separatists in this sense. But if human nature is viewed as entirely corrupt it follows that the conditions of regeneration must be supplied entirely from above. In so far as their uncompromising views of sin imply that the conditions of a good life are withdrawn from us, Luther and Calvin may be described as separatists, and, thus far, also may be named as predecessors of Barth.

Luther is a forerunner especially in that he regarded the whole nature of man as so corrupt that he can play no part whatever in receiving grace. He anathematized reason, and declared that "where the salvation of the soul is concerned, man is like the pillar of salt, like Lot's wife, yea like a block of wood and stone, that needs neither eyes, mouth, mind, nor heart."

Calvin allowed that we still retain some gifts of God in the corrupt state; but for him, as for Luther, the will is completely corrupt, so that it cannot resist the inclinations of our corrupt nature. Only an omnipotent act of grace, which renews the will despite its resistance, can restore us. Salvation and all good works are thus dependent on unconditional predestination, effectual grace springing from a decree of God which in the last analysis is arbitrary. Though, for Calvin, this decree is made once for all for every individual elected, whereas, for Barth, the divine decision is operative only from time to time, the two agree in turning finally to an arbitrary decision of God to explain how and when the conditions of true service are given us.

But it is precisely here that Calvin's system has been recognized as most open to criticism. Election cannot be arbitrary. It is significant that Calvin did not begin with the doctrine of predestination. As with Barth, the conception of God's way with sinners which this doctrine expresses is held as a corollary to the corruption of man's nature and his complete dependence on God for all the good that is in him. Without denying this dependence, Christian thought on God's way with sinners must start from the disclosure in Christ of a regenerating Love unceasingly extended to all. At this one point, Luther contrasts favourably with both Calvin and Barth. For he insists that the doctrine of predestination must be treated as a supplement to Christology, thereby recognizing that the revelation in Christ must determine how and when regeneration is made possible. He emphasized the point that the incarnation presupposes sin, holding that redemption is therein made for all. Thus, Calvin is a separatist, in that he excludes some from the grace that regenerates; Luther, in that he disqualifies human nature from co-operating with this grace.

A century later, Jansenism exemplifies separatism in every aspect. This movement is curious, in that it repudiates the ground of its origin. Arising out of continual protest against the intellectualism of Mediæval Theology, it ends by renouncing the natural life which brings into being the spiritual needs for which the simple heart finds the scholastic explanation of grace insufficient and unmeaning. According to St. Cyran, the regenerated sinner must be dead to all interests save God, even family ties being alien to the true religious life. Yet the movement developed logically enough from the principles of Augustine, Jansen's authority. Faith having nothing to do with reason, reason is renounced. From Augustine also comes the teaching that man is entirely dependent on God for release from a nature sinful throughout, his release and all good works being the result of irresistible grace with which he cannot co-operate.

The severance of the sphere of Christian living from our natural surroundings is pagan rather than Christian in origin, the precedent set by Augustine being perhaps accounted for partly by the violence of his conversion and partly by his former Manichæan connection. But the tendency to take dependence on God to mean that human nature cannot co-operate in the reception of grace seems to spring from Augustine and is common to his followers. And once synergism is denied in the reception of grace the ground is prepared for the denial of the sufficiency of the grace already offered in Christ. For the grace offered in Christ is not irresistible, but an appeal. The insufficiency of existing grace is implied in any doctrine of predestination. It is also expressly affirmed by the Jansenists, who declared that existing grace would have been sufficient for the state of innocence, but is insufficient for fallen human nature. Here, as in Barth, the point emphasized by Luther

THE WILL OF GOD AND THE CHRISTIAN METAPHYSIC

is overlooked, namely, that the incarnation is achieved expressly for sin.

But, unless a selective predestination is conceived to operate through the incarnation, Luther's negative anthropology makes it impossible to explain the diversity of the results it achieves among men. If this diversity is not to be explained as due to predestination in some form, it can be explained only by a doctrine of synergism which recognizes human responsibility in receiving grace as well as in living by its aid—a doctrine such as neither Augustine, Luther, Calvin, Jansen, nor Barth would allow; but such as is nevertheless implied in the appeal of Christ, who calls us to respond with heart, soul, strength, and mind. Christ looks for a response which goes far beyond anything reconcilable with the view of Kierkegaard, the most recent of Barth's predecessors. Kierkegaard's is the theology of redemption through a despair which persists throughout a Christian life, the moral aspect of which has been described as "the inward agony of finite man pressed down under his sense of the infinite God",[1] whereas redemption by Christ rescues us from despair, inspiring a morality of grateful and confident endeavour for the sake of Him who is to us a power and not a burden.

Among the biblical witnesses, John the Baptist could be claimed as a predecessor to Barth with greater justice than either St. Paul or Jeremiah. His declaration that the axe is laid to the root of the tree indicates an apocalyptic judgment of some kind, though it does not imply that human sin is incurable. His whole mission, also, is of the nature of a pointing finger: the mission assigned by Barth to all servants of God as well as to the written Word. His baptism with water unto repentance signified no more than a preparation for grace. But we must not forget that his mission was a special one, and declared to be so by himself. Nor must we forget how he was surprised by Christ's desire to be baptized by him, whereby He overrides the Baptist's abasement of his human service and unifies Himself with the religious endeavour of the community. While St. Paul deals with sin with uncompromising seriousness, he is at variance with Barth on essential points. That he did not believe in total depravity is evident from his declaration that the Gentiles do by nature the things contained in the Law, showing the work of the Law written in their hearts, their conscience bearing witness, though the Law has not been revealed to them (Rom. ii. 14–15). He appears also to vindicate human reason in affirming that invisible things, such as the power and eternity of God, are understood by the things that are made (Rom. i. 20). As we have seen, his teaching on spirituality and the Christ after

[1] H. R. Mackintosh, *Types of Modern Theology*, p. 251, note.

the flesh is not in agreement with the Barthian view. Lastly, St. Paul believed that by the grace which he received through Christ he could impart spiritual gifts to those under his care, by his own labours, to the end that they might be established (Rom. i. 11).

Jeremiah is not the only one in the Old Testament who believed that man could sin beyond redemption. But, whatever affinity Barth may claim to possess with Jeremiah, the similarity breaks down at the one point which matters supremely: which is, the relation of the sinful servant to the God he serves. Jeremiah recognized that the sincere intent necessary for the performance of his duty might at times be lacking, but he did not believe that sin destroyed his capacity to hear and obey the Word of God. "If thou shalt take forth the precious from the vile, thou shalt be as my mouth." The witnesses to revelation in the past may warn us to expect a future self-relation of God to us. But they certainly do warn us that His self-relation is already abidingly in operation; that it is God who awaits our response to it; and that this is the part that falls to us in the consummation of His divine purpose.

www.ingramcontent.com/pod-product-compliance
Lightning Source LLC
Chambersburg PA
CBHW051108160426
43193CB00010B/1369